Grounding Our Faith
in a Pluralist World

Grounding Our Faith
in a Pluralist World

—with a little help from Nāgārjuna

by

JOHN P. KEENAN

with

SYDNEY COPP, LANSING DAVIS, AND BUSTER G. SMITH

WIPF & STOCK · Eugene, Oregon

GROUNDING OUR FAITH IN A PLURALIST WORLD
—with a little help from Nāgārjuna

Wipf & Stock
A Division of Wipf and Stock Publishers
199 W. 8th Ave., Suite 3
Eugene, OR 97401

www.wipfandstock.com

ISBN 13: 978-1-55635-997-2

Manufactured in the U.S.A.

Table of Contents

Acknowledgments

THREE STUDENTS WHO STUDIED with me in the Department of Religion at Middlebury College—Sydney Copp, Lansing Davis, and Buster G. Smith, all now graduates for some years—became so engaged in questions treated here that each chose to work on some aspect of this topic for a senior thesis. My Middlebury colleague E. Burke Rochford, Jr., a professor of religion and sociology who has written on Hare Krishna as well as on the interfaith encounter, graciously agreed to take on some of their thesis supervision while I was on leave. I am grateful for the efforts of these four individuals, who provided impetus and raw material for this endeavor.

I would also like to express my gratitude to Professor Paul F. Knitter of Union Theological Seminary and Dr. William R. Burrows, General Editor of Orbis Books, for their critical reading and brotherly evaluation of the text.

Acknowledgments

Preface

How in this world today can we affirm the faith that is in us—the faith handed down by our mothers and fathers, or another faith that we ourselves have sought and embraced—how can we affirm one faith and still remain radically open to the many other religious traditions in our world that claim, and indeed demonstrate in practice, their own validity as authentic guides for human living and dying?

How can we acknowledge the truths of many different faiths without denigrating the power of any one particular faith to convert and transform the lives of its followers?

How can we, from our limited perspective within a particular grounded faith tradition, understand other religions or adjudicate among them? Should we even try? Is it possible that our religions are only as culturally valid as our racial or ethnic identities? Are they something to be cherished, but in no way to be promoted to super-historical status?

These are questions that urge themselves upon members of any religious tradition who are committed to practicing their own faith but at the same time aware of the competing truth claims of different religions practiced among their neighbors and around the globe.

A multiplicity of religious faiths is not new. Nor are these questions new. What is perhaps new is that more and more people are willing to grant that valuable insights can be found in traditions other than their own. And those other traditions confront us with their own efficacious spiritual paths of practice, their canons of scriptures, and their own immense body of tradition. Today's issue is existentially poignant, more so than the classical confrontations between Christian and Jewish traditions vis-à-vis the pagan world and its philosophies.

We have today come a long way from the exclusivistic denial that any truth could possibly exist in other people's religions. Many have even moved beyond the stance of inclusivism, the acknowledgment that other faith traditions may incorporate at least *some* of our own truth. In recent decades, in fact, a rather large number of people have adopted the attitude of "pluralism," which is the affirmation that a number of different religious traditions are indeed valid.

But there is a downside to the open-minded, pluralistic view: It has a tendency to lead people to doubt the importance of identifying with, or fully participating in, any faith tradition. If one tradition is just as valid as another, then what is the point of committing ourselves to any of them? In other words, a stance of religious pluralism can potentially lead to an attitude of "whatever." If all religions are equally true and meaningful, some wonder, are they not just as equally meaningless?

I would submit, and it is the argument of this book, that we human beings possess no adequate viewpoint that can give us a paradigm for understanding the plurality of religious traditions. The discipline known as history of religions can study religions as phenomena of human life, but only at an objectifying distance, only at arm's length. By intentionally bracketing issues of truth—setting such matters aside as inappropriate for scholarly consideration—the study of religions cannot raise or treat the conflict between an individual's commitment to a particular faith and his or her awareness of the multiplicity of faiths. Commitment to a particular religious tradition, by the very intensity of that commitment, favors that faith above all others and tends to regard those others as somewhat suspect, or at least alien. How then can we proceed without insisting on some faith-abandoning neutrality?

What follows is not an argument for or against any specific theological or doctrinal viewpoint. It is rather a suggestion for changing the nature of the present interfaith discussion—its purview, its ground, its premise, its philosophical tenets. The approach recommended here would emphasize the limits of human knowing and would question the nature of questioning itself, to the end of grounding us each with intense commitment in our own vernacular faith tradition while at the same time opening us radically to the rich panoply of our neighbors' faiths.

As an aid to this project of developing a new interfaith philosophy, I propose to employ Mahāyāna Buddhist thought, specifically its philosophy of mind and understanding, which can serve us well in considering issues of faith commitment and expressed truth. "Mahāyāna" means the Great (Sanskrit *mahā*) Vehicle (*yāna*) of Buddhism. This is the branch of Buddhism that is prevalent in East Asia. Its philosophies are indeed "philosophy" in the most literal sense of our term, for their central concern or affinity (Greek *philos*) is for awakening—that is, wisdom (*sophia*). Indeed, the goal of the Mahāyāna path is wisdom. Mahāyāna thought addresses itself to all who have minds and who seek to understand.

Although Mahāyāna philosophy originated within the Buddhist tradition, it can support any tradition that would attempt to explicate faith in understanding. Its nuanced approach to religious thinking reveals that all our usual attitudes toward other people's faiths—exclusivism, inclusivism, even pluralism—are inadequate, in that they are grounded in our conscious or unconscious preconceptions of just how the universe fits together. Our common, though often unacknowledged, metaphysical assumptions determine the vantage point from which we regard other faiths. These assumptions in turn are based upon the necessity of having *some* vantage point from which to survey and arrange this world of many faiths.

Mahāyāna philosophy will bring these assumptions of ours into question, confronting us with the limitations of human viewpoints and even of human language. It will lead us to realize that we must abandon our bloated claims to having captured truth in language, to having seen the big picture of reality. It can then finally bring us back around to a radical commitment to the power and truth of our own particular and grounded faith tradition, and at the same time encourage us toward a radical openness to, and respect for, the traditions of others.

At the same time, because such an approach serves the truth without pretended claims of capturing the one and only truth, each of us in our different traditions are freed to develop apologetic, and indeed missionary, approaches for our traditions that both recommend our faith and learn from the faiths of others. We all need to give reasoned accounts of the faith that is in us, and those reasoned accounts will depend on philosophies of human faith and understanding in all its languaged and cultured diversity. Apologetics endeavors to "defend" faith as a valid and authentic human commitment, while missionary efforts recommend that faith to others for their personal consideration.

In virtue of my own history, I am grounded in the Christian tradition and that since my infancy. I was raised in Roman Catholic schools and trained in the scriptures and traditions in a Catholic seminary; I now serve as a part-time priest in an Episcopal Church in the northernmost reaches of Vermont. Since the late 1960s I have been attracted to Buddhist thought and doctrine. After seminary, I studied Chinese language and philosophy at the University of Pennsylvania, and then Buddhist traditions at the University of Wisconsin—to the point of identifying with Mahāyāna philosophy. I have many mentors in both the Christian and Buddhist traditions and am deeply grateful to all. This double orientation accounts for a greater emphasis on these two traditions in the pages that follow. In truth, this book is the work of a Christian theologian addressing primarily other Christians, but I hope that the Buddhist philosophy of faith offered herein may be helpful as well to people of other religious traditions.

A note to readers: In this volume we will extract and employ for our purposes some of the fundamental tenets of Buddhist philosophy. For a full introduction to Buddhism as a many-faceted religious tradition see, for example, the Mahāyāna philosophy of Gadjin M. Nagao, the contemporary Buddhist meditations and essays of David Loy, and the Zen writings of Ruben Habito.

John P. Keenan
Newport, Vermont

1

A World of Many Faiths

When Faith Meets Faith[1]

OUR ANCESTORS IN THE rural communities and city streets of the Western world, like those in villages and metropolises around the globe, lived primarily within bounded worlds of monocultural assumptions—assumptions that supported, and were supported by, a particular religious faith and practice.

They of course did sometimes encounter people of other faith traditions but did not often speak with them about religion. Let sleeping theologies lie, they seemed to think. Disagreements indeed there were, even between different denominations of the same faith tradition—here Catholic and Protestant, conservative and liberal, Orthodox and Reformed, there Sunni and Shiite, Nichiren and Zen. Still, within each religious culture and neighborhood there was broad agreement on a common set of philosophical assumptions about the oneness of truth and the nature of authentic practice. There was no need to discuss differences, for the possession of religious truth allowed one to remain insular within the shared overarching pattern of a common cultural life of faith and practice.

That is to say, things remained, and still do remain, harmonious wherever a cultural pattern of arm's length religious tolerance is the norm. We build on the work of our ancestors, and Western culture has over time developed a broad consensus about tolerance toward the faith traditions of others. And so here in the West, even when incompletely enunciated, culturally irenic assumptions remain potent. Several centuries ago, our ancestors may have burned one another at the stake over words in a

---

1. With a nod to Orbis Books' *Faith Meets Faith* series.

prayer book, but in this culture we have by now been schooled to live and let live, religiously speaking.

Nevertheless, truth still tends to be regarded as univocal so that any viewpoint is seen as either true or false. Co-religionists of other denominations or sects who profess an alternative understanding of our faith are thus looked upon, however unfortunately, as unfortunate. But patiently they are left to work out their salvation on their own. As for altogether different religions and foreign cultures, until recently these were far away, had little to do with our native culture, and were dismissed as obviously false (although possibly possessed of a grain or two of truth mixed into their morass of error). In today's society, many such alien faiths have moved closer, into our cities and even sometimes into our neighborhoods. They are seen perhaps as simply unavoidably different, but their adherents are fellow citizens so long as they too affirm the overarching norms of cultural tolerance. No longer pagans, heathens, outsiders, infidels, or gentiles to one another, we must all practice our faith within a context of civilized tolerance.

The picture of the culturally bounded societies of our forbearers, each neatly conjoined to its particular religious tradition, has never been entirely true, of course—because the assumption of culturally well-defined traditions and independent religions is not true. Each and every tradition of faith, and each and every philosophic set of affirmations, has influenced others and has itself been influenced by a myriad of external factors.

Buddhism grew from within a Hindu worldview, and doctrines of transmigration, karma, and awakening are the common property of these two major traditions. Christian doctrine was grounded upon the Hebrew Scriptures, although it was regarded as the consummation of the Hebrews' earlier covenant with God and did reinterpret notions of the Torah through the new revelation of Jesus.[2] *The Upanishads* of India, which seem to have influenced the Greek philosopher Plotinus, may well have exerted a pull on his Neoplatonism and in turn had an effect upon early Jewish and Christian mysticism. Muslims accept Moses and Jesus as prophets leading up to Muhammad. They also have a tender devotion

---

2. Davies and Allison, *Gospel According to Saint Matthew*, 2:296, on Matt 11:25, which states that Jesus "fulfills the calling of Israel, embodying in his own person Torah and Wisdom and thus making known the perfect will of God."

to Mary, the mother of Jesus (in contrast to Christian Protestants, who eschew such devotion as too "Roman").

Pure Land Buddhist Japanese immigrants in Hawaii and California, seeking to be culturally American, for a time called their places of worship "churches" rather than "temples," introduced organ music, installed pews, and formed Buddhist Youth Fellowships on the model of Protestant youth groups. Such historical influences of one religious tradition upon another have been far-reaching and in some instances surprising: The rosary was probably used first by Buddhists, adopted by Muslims as prayer beads, and then propagated among Roman Catholics by the mendicant and learned preacher St. Dominic (1170–1221), as an aid to meditation and a symbol of the true Christian faith.

Despite such mutual and global influences and regardless of the all-embracing modern culture of tolerance, religious traditions do tend to incarnate themselves within specific ethnicities and particular geographies, to identify boundaries, and to serve as the ground upon which groups of people define their reality and order their world. Often they are tied to sacred places and arise within some sacred geography. We humans are, as Genesis teaches, earthlings (*ādām*), from the earth (*ādāmā*) and located not globally everywhere, but in some neighborhood or other. Indeed, we feel compelled to construct localized functional worlds in order to live together, to live at all.

Times do change and sometimes a religion will come to be viewed as insufficient or invalid, an old superstition that needs to yield to a more enlightened awareness. Even then, its practitioners will likely feel compelled to seek some new path over familiar ground along which to reorganize their lives and avoid chaos and meaninglessness. In times of plenty and prosperity, the "old-time" religion may enjoy broad, if sometimes shallow, acceptance within the culture. But in periods of distress and suffering, the same religion may wither and die.

Or, in times of stress, a religion may—and often does—develop militant orientations, eschatological visions of a better future, and revolutionary justifications for political resistance in the name of faith. Violence is a common human response to distress and fear. It may be directed inward, in rejection of an accepted tradition, or outward, toward forces that threaten a still cherished religious faith. But, when faith and life itself appear to be threatened by primordial chaos and death, violence will seek a religious warrant.[3] As Karl Barth knew so well, we human beings create religion to keep the chaos at bay.

In some cases, a religious tradition faced with challenges will eschew an extreme reaction and instead launch upon a creative effort to reclaim the ground of that faith, coming home to the cultural landscape of its source. This entails going to ground in its revelations, for faith comes from the revealing impetus of the Spirit, of the Buddha realm, of God, through seers and prophets, from the awakened ones. In my neighborhood, it came from the Holy Spirit. But all religions with equal vigor proclaim themselves to be founded upon primal experiences and revealed manifestations of deep insight into life and truth. We humans nurture those basic revelations within our particular cultures and languages so that they grow over time into traditions that serve as barriers against the ever-present possibility of chaos and meaninglessness.

Sadly and frequently, however, in our commitment to revelation, we forget that it is we ourselves who have received these revelations, that it is we humans who have nurtured and recorded them, forming them into the monuments of elegance and truth that they are. By the very receiving of revelation, we mold and construct our understanding and our society. But in our urgent desire to affirm absolute and unconditioned truth, often we fail to acknowledge that our revealed worldviews are in fact also the cultural products of human endeavor. We want to proclaim the truth to be wholly and just-as-it-is revealed: God speaks, and we but listen, thrilled by the happy fact that God speaks our language.

Confident that our religion as practiced is fixed and formulated by such revelation, we human beings forget that we ourselves are the creators of religious institutions and conventions, and indeed of language itself. In consequence, we lose any sense that our religion can change its structure if so desired.[4] This kind of believing creates bastions of forgetful comfort, which underpin our life as lived and protect us alike from states of mental instability and from life insight. We assiduously seek such comfortable havens of certainty, because, as philosopher and sociologist Émile Durkheim observed, when religion "no longer fulfills its function ... confusion and uneasiness result."[5] Fearing that unease, we replace think-

---

3. Berger, *Sacred Canopy*, 22–23.

4. Berger, *Sacred Canopy*, 87.

5. Pickering, *Durkheim's Sociology*, 307.

ing with faith. It is then that violence may show itself as the shadow side of religious conviction.

Although, undeniably, violence may, and does, sometimes appear as the dark side of religious commitment, the faith traditions—when practiced authentically—shine forth with the muted light of human endeavor. At their best, they strive to remain true to the inherited faith while drawing from their sacred writings new insights, ever more faithfully, in ever changing cultural circumstances, addressing ever new crises and opportunities.

But the task of addressing new circumstances has become more and more difficult. In a modern world where we are so aware of many different religions, the very plurality of faiths threatens our sense of stability and calls into question our own accepted sureties. This is our new crisis—and our new opportunity. The way in which we react to multiple truth systems can determine whether or not we can maintain our sense of religious place within our own tradition, and this in turn affects faith and practice. Some indeed may abandon faith altogether—either by rejecting what they now regard as a narrow-minded practice, or conversely by making faith itself into an absolute.

Awareness of a multiplicity of religions threatens any given tradition, and so throughout history we human beings have employed a variety of strategies to keep at bay the insistent awareness that our faith is in fact molded and formed within a cultural framework. Even though our tradition may be revealed, the terms in which it is expressed depend upon human ideas and orientations that are not themselves a part of the revelation.

As noted above, three broad approaches have been employed to address this vexing problem of many religions: The first is a sweeping, often exclusive, dismissal that does not bother much with trying to understand the other traditions. A more inclusive approach seeks to account for other faiths within a theological understanding of one's own faith. The pluralist position—increasingly popular—recognizes the richness of other traditions and confesses that many different paths are equally valid and true.[6]

---

6. See Race, *Christians and Religious Pluralism*, for the typology of approaches. Knitter, *Theologies of Religions*, offers a fourth, "acceptance model," 173–237.

Exclusivism: possessing the true picture

In the past—and continuing into the present—a common strategy employed by deeply committed religious adherents when dealing with the multiplicity of religious beliefs has been simply to reject the foreign as false and to live one's own faith in pretended cultural isolation. However, such a pretense requires us to ignore the cultural roots of our own religion while purporting to possess an unsullied and pure faith that is in no way a human construct.

The early Christian theologian Tertullian (c. 160–225) asked rhetorically and dismissively, "What has Jerusalem [the Christian faith that superseded Judaism] to do with Athens [the Greek philosophic traditions that in fact set the cultural framework for all Christian thinking]?" Perhaps Tertullian was able to maintain such a viewpoint in the limited sphere of his world, but Greek philosophy and critique were saliently present in that world. He was not happy about that, and that is why he wished to disassociate himself from them. Later Christians who had any knowledge at all of the development of Christian thought could not pretend to ignore either their Jewish roots or the Greek philosophy through which the Fathers of the Christian Church had articulated Christian doctrine. Likewise, modern Christians in a world with so many centers ignore the cultural roots of their own and other religious traditions only at the expense of a crippled understanding of themselves and others.

Examples abound of our human proclivity to shut out things that are foreign and uncomfortable. Once a graduate school professor of mine, a specialist in Chinese art, was on a guided tour of Christian paintings in Rome when the docent pointed out an image of the "first religious nun." "But," my teacher objected, "there were nuns in China *long* before that time!" The docent shot back without a moment's hesitation, "I mean *real* nuns!" No one else in the group objected, for it was obvious to all that a Chinese Buddhist nun did not qualify as a "real" nun and therefore did not have to be counted. Perhaps today someone in the group might indeed take exception, for more of us are aware that there really are—and long have been—Buddhist nuns in China and elsewhere.

We now live at the beginning of a millennium that is characterized by insistent, and at times unsettling, reminders that there are in this world many different religions, and that to all intents and purposes they function quite as well for their believers as ours does for us. We are coming to

6

see that we need not replace these religions with our own, that perhaps we do not need to convert the whole world to our own faith. This certainly does not mean that we, each in our grounded faith, would not witness to that faith and would not preach it to all and sundry, everywhere. But we have no need to arrogate our culturally rooted theologies above the similarly but differently culture-bound faith traditions of others.

This is not a theological judgment but simply an empirical observation, clear to anyone who travels this world and lives for a time among people of other cultures and other faiths. The obverse can be argued only by ignoring the common sense of the many people who have lived among Hindus, Buddhists, Muslims, Christians, Jews, Taoists, Zoroastrians, and all manner of other believers and found them to be brothers and sisters with genuine human and moral sensitivities. Indeed it is this new postmillennial awareness that, far from resolving the matter, bluntly raises the issue of cultural and religious relativity. It forces us to ask how we can denigrate other religions as untrue and inauthentic when we simply know nothing about them. The exclusivist's insistence that he or she has the one and only truth sins against the norm of cultural tolerance, against who we are and whom our ancestors have made us to be.

To make matters worse for true Christian believers,[7] experience shows that any acknowledgment of the plurality of authentically practiced traditions will bend the question back onto what used to be narrowly Christian issues. This bending back will occur over and over again, for any opening to other faith traditions will necessarily lead Christians to reconsider issues of revelation and faith, of Western culture and Jesus. What does it mean to claim, as does Karl Barth (despite his views that *all* religion is defiled as a human construct of arrogance and pride), that revelation from God is only through Jesus? Or what about others who claim a revelation from Allah that asserts Christian beliefs about Jesus are false?

Or, if one understands the Pure Land Buddhist teaching of Shinran—according to which we are saved not by our own power but only through the grace-laden other-power of the Buddha Amida—how can one recommend the exclusivist claim that God, who is totally other, saves only through faith in Christ? The structure of salvation in Shin Pure Land Buddhism parallels Luther and Barth, but the mover is not God

7. Hoffner, *True Believer*, 58–90.

in Jesus but rather Amida Buddha through his world-transcendent and encompassing vow.[8] How can one study that faith tradition without recognizing the very same theological structure and indeed the very same discourse on grace there as here?

Is it any wonder that exclusivists practice a studied ignorance of other traditions? To learn more deeply of those traditions might undermine their narrow understanding of faith. And so they choose to remain ignorant.

Inclusivism: possessing the complete picture

A second option for dealing with a plurality of religions—more gentle than simply rejecting them as false—has been to regard alien traditions as partial truths that have—or may in the future—come to their fulfillment within one's own faith. Thus Christians demoted the Hebrew Scriptures to the designation of "old" covenant, or "Old Testament," while Christian texts became the "new" covenant, the "New Testament." This despite the fact that the term "new covenant" was first used by the Hebrew prophet Jeremiah in the fifth century before Christ, to describe the Torah that is written not on tablets of stone but on the hearts of men and women, the men and women of Israel.

This type of inclusive strategy, wherever it is found—and it is found almost everywhere—brushes aside the original context of others' religious traditions or their sacred writings. It creates updated or truer traditions, or perhaps simply rereads the other in terms that are more familiar. Islam takes a step beyond Judaism and Christianity by following the austere and elegant faith in one God Allah and trusting in the last and greatest of his prophets, Muhammad. The Qur'an then becomes the filter through which Muslims read both the Hebrew Scriptures sacred to Judaism and New Testament of the Christians. At each stage in this kind of process, the newer religious community sees itself as superseding and completing the older one. And although they may look to a new revelation as the source of their own authority, they will commonly teach that revelation—and thus religious warranty—ends at some point. For Christians, that point is the close of the Christian canon. For Muslims, revelation ends with the prophet Muhammad, and so Islam rejects the later Baha'i revelations of

---

8. See Unno's *Tannishō*, with its English translation of, and concise introduction to, this important Pure Land text.

Baha' Ullāh, for by definition there can be no prophet who supersedes Muhammad.

Inclusivist strategies are not limited to later traditions fulfilling earlier ones. Buddhists teach that the culmination of truth, no matter where located in time, is found in the Buddhist scriptures, and that other traditions, earlier or later, are only "skillful means" for teaching karmically less intelligent and perspicacious people. Modern Buddhists do not reject other traditions, but they often do regard them as but steps toward the fullness of Buddhist teaching.[9] Taoists do the same thing, identifying the Buddha as an earlier appearance of their own Chinese progenitor Lao-tzu, an appearance that was tailor-made for the less adept people of barbarian India.

Christian examples of such a graded-inclusive approach—which grades other traditions as lesser examples of one's own perfected faith— are both ancient and modern. Justin Martyr (d. 165 CE) in *The Second Apology* argues that the Word, incarnate in Jesus of Nazareth, had implanted itself in the minds of all philosophers and thinkers since the beginning of human history. Thus even ancient philosophers express, however imperfectly, the truth that is fully revealed only in Jesus, the Word made flesh. According to Justin, even before Jesus, the Greek philosophers Plato and Aristotle, Plotinus (205–270 CE) and Philo (c. 20 BCE–50 CE) had all participated in the wisdom of the Word of God. Justin writes:

> I confess that I both boast and with all my strength strive to be found a Christian—not because the teachings of Plato are different from those of Christ, but because they are not in all respects similar, as neither are those of the others, Stoics, and poets, and historians. For each man spoke well in proportion to the share he had of the seminal word, seeing what was related to it. But those who contradict themselves on the more important points appear not to have possessed the heavenly (i.e., dimly seen at a distance) wisdom, and the knowledge which cannot be spoken against. Whatever things were rightly said among all men, are the property of us Christians. For next to God, we worship and love the Word who is from the

9. Dalai Lama, *Beyond Dogma*, 181–215. Also of interest is the work of Katsumi Takizawa, a Japanese Christian theologian who studied with Karl Barth. Takizawa accepted Barth's description of all religions as deluded and idolatrous human constructs and affirmed the otherness of revelation, but he extended that otherness to Buddhist teachings such as Shin Pure Land. He wrote an interesting commentary entitled *Tannishō to Gendai* [The Tannishō and the Modern Age].

unbegotten and ineffable God, since He also became man for our sakes, that, becoming a partaker of our sufferings, He might also bring us healing. For all the writers were able to see realities darkly through the sowing of the implanted Word that was in them. For the seed and imitation imparted according to capacity is one thing, and quite another is the thing itself, of which there is the participation and imitation according to the grace which is from Him.[10]

Justin Martyr's is the earliest instance of a Christian inclusive theology of religions, expressing the idea that other traditions are to be regarded as having a little bit—some more, some less—of the truth that is fully revealed in Christ. But we must reject his ploy of regarding all "pagans" in terms of the Christian doctrine of the Incarnate Word. Indeed, pagan thinkers Plato and the Stoics would have seen Christ not as the fulfillment of all their questioning, but rather as a less philosophically mature version of their own love of wisdom.

A similar approach has been practiced in our time by Karl Rahner, a leading Catholic theologian, who argued that all non-Christians—to the extent that they understand and practice truth—are in fact sharing in the reality of Christ, even though they are unaware of the true name of that truth. He called these people "anonymous" Christians for if they could but realize the full truth of the gospel, they would consciously identify themselves as Christians. Sadly, in his view, culture and history often preclude that recognition.[11]

Contemporary theologian Jacques Dupuis employs Justin's model to affirm that the truth-revealing word may be found in other traditions, arguing convincingly that true revelation does not cease with the coming of the incarnate Word in Jesus.[12] Stephen Kaplan argues that different paths lead to different summits, each tradition limning its summit within its particular culture and tradition.[13]

In a similar vein, S. Mark Heim grounds the validity of many traditions upon Christian reflections on the inner life of God as three distinct persons, demonstrating thereby that each tradition has its own valid and efficacious intended salvation—perhaps cessation (*nirvāṇa*) or union with God. In intense awareness of others, one may deepen insight into,

10. Roberts and Donaldson, *Ante-Nicene Fathers*, 1:192–93.

11. See Rahner, "Anonymous Christians," in *Theological Investigations*, 6:295–312.

12. Dupuis, *Toward A Christian Theology*, 57–60 and 243.

13. Kaplan, *Different Paths, Different Summits*.

and committed practice of, one's native faith. At the same time, one encounters those other faiths as valid and efficacious, although leading to
distinctly different salvations. One can, he asserts, be both committed and
tolerant, embracing "the other" as brother or sister.[14]

For some Buddhists, the *Lotus Scripture* constitutes a classical and
structurally parallel approach to Justin Martyr's kind of all-embracing
and irenic inclusivism. This scripture, dating somewhat later than Justin,
declares in the voice of the Buddha that Buddhist teachings other than
the full truth of the One Vehicle that is presented in that scripture are
designed as tactful, expedient approaches to be preached to less prepared
persons on a level—invariably lower—appropriate to their understanding. But the *Lotus Scripture* makes no bones about the fact that there is
nevertheless only the One Vehicle of the Buddha, for all teachings of the
faith traditions lead to the one goal of Buddha awakening:

> [T]he Tathāgatas [i.e., the Buddhas] have only a single Buddha ve-
> hicle which they employ in order to preach the teaching to living
> beings. They do not have any other vehicle, a second or a third one
> . . . . The Buddhas of the past used countless numbers of expedi-
> ent means, various causes and conditions, and words of simile and
> parable in order to expound the doctrines for the sake of living be-
> ings. These doctrines are all for the sake of the one Buddha vehicle.
> These living beings, by listening to the doctrine of the Buddhas, are
> all eventually able to attain wisdom embracing all species.[15]

This passage and others in the *Lotus Scripture* clearly make the point
that all approaches other than the One Vehicle are but tactful adjustments
to the life-situations of people who are not yet ready to hear and understand the One Vehicle of full and perfect awakening. However, at the end
of the day of transmigration, all people will ride that single Buddha vehicle to Buddha awakening, abandoning their foolish adherence to lesser
paths and lesser goals.

The *Lotus Scripture* was not, however, addressing itself to questions
of religious pluralism here. From beginning to end, it remained within
the context of intramural argumentation among Buddhists. This text
exalts the One Vehicle of the Eternal Buddha while demoting the final
validity of the two "lesser" vehicles—those of the faithful "hearer" of the

---

14. First enunciated in Heim, *Salvations*, and then in his *Depth of the Riches*.
15. Watson, *Lotus Sūtra*, 31.

word of Buddha and of the "solitary enlightened" hermit in his anchorite withdrawal. Unable to deny the textual record of a tradition in which earlier scriptures portray the Buddha as offering other, different teachings, it employs the notion of "skillful means" to account for these differences—for all are embraced in the One Vehicle. Even if we do not know about the Buddha ideal, "all unconsciously we ourselves may be walking that Way."[16]

It would be but a short jump, however, for adherents of the *Lotus Scripture* to apply the same strategy to the teachings of non-Buddhist religious traditions. But when Buddhists did engage in controversy with non-Buddhist traditions in ancient India, they did not, I think, often appeal to the notion of skillful means; they simply refuted the Hindu schools as false and perverse.[17] As far as I am aware, classical Buddhist Mahāyāna texts commonly confine their argument to their own doctrinal context, on the assumption that Buddhism alone—with its teachings of emptiness and dependent arising, ultimate and conventional truth—is adequate and accurate.

In modern times, the One Vehicle doctrine of the *Lotus Scripture*—the all-inclusiveness of Buddhist teaching expressed through various skillful means—has become a characteristic of Mahāyāna Buddhist movements that are much more globally aware. These groups employ strategies that are less graded and dismissive, more embracing and theologically sensitive. The Risshō Kōsei Kai and the Sōka Gakkai—two modern Japanese Buddhist movements based on the *Lotus Scripture*—interpret this scripture's teaching on skillful means to argue that there are many "vehicles" to salvation, all of which are accommodations to a silent truth.

Nikkyō Niwano, founder of the Risshō Kōsei Kai, distinguishes the One Vehicle not as the single true vehicle in contrast to the lesser vehicles,

---

16. See Niwano, *Guide to the Threefold Lotus Sutra*, 47. He comments on the parable of the burning house, wherein the deluded children "who thought only that they would get goat carts, deer carts, and bullock carts, were all alike given the unexpected pleasure of a great white bullock cart, the best possible: the way to Buddhahood itself." Again, Niwano teaches that "[the Lotus practice] is the one Way, apart from all others, that humanity should pursue," 39.

17. As an example of such a polemic, see Dharmapāla's and Candrakīrti's critique of heretical views in Tillemans, *Āryadeva, Dharmapāla, and Candrakīrti*, 1:85–135, which for the most part proceeds by reasoned argument but occasionally denigrates Brahmans as shrewd and stealthy inventors of the ancient Veda scriptures, deceivers, and tricksters (108–9).

but as an ultimate vehicle "to be followed equally by all people."[18] This Buddhist theology moves toward a universal embracing of other traditions in religious gentleness, accepting them as variously skillful teachings toward that "supreme teaching, that is, the enlightenment of the one Buddha-vehicle, . . . shining brilliantly."[19]

Also gently inclusivist, the Tibetan Dalai Lama recommends that each person practice his or her own tradition of faith, because all religions offer needed comfort along the path to enlightenment. He reassures us that there is no need for all to convert to Buddhism. And yet, the context of this Dge Lugs Pa recommendation is the ancient teaching that we transmigrate from life to life so that, in the end—innumerable lifetimes perhaps from here—we all may embrace the true Buddhist teaching and thus be enlightened.[20] The Dalai Lama's irenic and all-encompassing approach is theologically grounded in this clear, ascertainable Buddhist doctrine.

Gentle though they may be, these forms of more or less graded inclusivism—whether Buddhist or Christian, whether expressed by the Dalai Lama or the Pope—are today decidedly unskillful and untactful strategies to employ in the encounter between religions. Such approaches disable their own proponents from engaging in genuine dialogue with others, for they have already classified those others as possessing but some inferior version of the truth as found in full in the Buddhist scriptures, or the Bible, or the Qur'an. Graded inclusivism by its nature assumes that one's own religion without any doubt possesses the true and valid norm in reference to which all other faiths are to be ranked. Although this stance moves beyond the exclusivists' arrogant confidence that they alone have access to truth and reaches toward embracing the full plurality of traditions, it often wobbles in indecision about the next move.

This inclusivist attitude entails deep and, I would maintain, insoluble problems. By adjudicating other traditions, indeed even by embracing

18. Niwano, *Buddhism for Today*, xv.

19. Niwano, "Realm of the One Vehicle," 43: "I have met with people of religion from around the world. From speaking with those who are leaders of their respective faiths, I have learned that in the original, basic essence of religion, that is, a belief in God or the Buddha, all faiths are in basic agreement, even if they express it using different terms."

20. Discussion with José Cabezón. It is also simple common sense that a faith that holds that we pass through innumerable lifetimes is in no great rush to convert people right here and now, as compared, for instance, to Christians, whose eschaton looms more definitively.

them, it also embraces a cultural and theological arrogance that assumes one's own history, one's own religion and its scriptures, or one's own mystic philosophy, as the norm by which all others are to be measured. My own religion, it just so happens, is scripturally based and thus true for, among all the competing alternatives, at the origin and heart of faith, it is the one that embraces all. Thank God (or Buddha), it is mine! Such an attitude, and its consequent theology, is supremely unskillful. Moreover, its proponents often are gravely deficient in their understanding—even ignorant—of the traditions they would demote, for the obvious reason that they are convinced they already have full access to the truth within their own cultural web of meaning. Gentle dialogues do indeed occur, yet apparently inclusivists feel little or no need to learn in depth or detail about the other *from* the other.

In this small world of the twenty-first century, we must perforce live and deal peacefully and respectfully with people of many different religious traditions. Precisely because the inclusivist views described above are based on theologies specific to single traditions, they wind up, no matter how or when, failing to meet others as true brothers and sisters. These approaches are culturally condescending, and as such they will not do.

How do we get beyond inclusivism?

And so we still have a problem. We face a challenge that our ancestors, cocooned defensively if unconsciously within their cultures, were not forced to meet. Indeed, this era of multiple religious truths drives some to pine for a return to those good old days of a bounded cultural world where we might proclaim that true religion just is what it is.[21] And many are wary, moreover, that dialogue among religions will dilute all into a common and tasteless soup.

But whatever the difficulties inherent in regarding other religions without condescension or rejection, and however debatable the fruits of interfaith dialogue and theology, religious thinkers today still must grapple with this crucial question: How theologically do we account for the very existence of other faith traditions that we now acknowledge to be doctrinally sophisticated and existentially profound?[22]

21. Ratzinger, *Truth and Tolerance*, 66–69, where he argues that Christianity is itself a culture, and not simply a faith to be enculturated.

22. *Pace* Ratzinger, *Truth and Tolerance*, 85–89. Also note, 176, where the pagan phi-

This question cannot be ignored, for in our modern culture of tolerance, the very awareness of other religious traditions worthy of respect
has for some individuals become an obstacle to faith. It is what I would
call a "gateway" issue. If thoughtful people do not see in a particular faith
community an appreciative and affirming understanding of *other* faiths,
then for them this becomes a barrier to embarking upon, or continuing in,
the practice of faith. Unless this dilemma is resolved so that members of
one faith tradition may embrace a tolerant and respectful attitude toward
others, it will effectively discourage people from committing themselves
to any specific religious practice.

Not so many years ago, Christian mission theology frequently re-
ferred to "preparation for the gospel," the minimal social and economic
conditions that were necessary for people to be able to hear the gospel
and commit themselves to its path. That theme has receded, for being
poor does not in fact prevent faith from taking hold of people. But new,
cultural barriers to faith commitment have arisen—the awareness of
multiple and beautiful faith traditions with intriguing practices and theologies and breathtaking art and architecture, coupled with a widespread
conviction that to be authentically human means to be tolerant. Thus, in
our day, unless a faith community is open to the world, the entire world,
many will be reluctant to commit heart and soul to the religious tradition
that it commends.

And so we have moved away from old models of self-enclosed classical cultures and become ever more aware of the diversity of ways of
being religiously human.[23] How are we now to regard the truth claims

---

losopher Symmachus is paralleled with modern universalists, for he too contended that
all religious ideas and images represented in different ways the self-same reality. But the
present awareness of a multiplicity of traditions urges upon us a new and different challenge, for these traditions are recognized, indeed partially but nevertheless truly, from
the inside by sympathetic readings of their scriptures and friendly conversations with
their practitioners. They are known to us, not as merely philosophic ideas, but as richly
textured traditions that insist only on engaged thinking and committed practice.

23. Lonergan, *Doctrinal Pluralism*, 4–9 and 56–65. See especially 9: "To confine the
Catholic Church to a classicist mentality is to keep the Catholic Church out of the modern world and to prolong an already too long prolonged crisis within the Church." And
29: "Scholastic theology was a monumental achievement. Its influence on the Church has
been profound and enduring. Up to Vatican II, which preferred a more biblical turn of
speech, it has provided much of the background whence proceeded pontifical documents
and conciliar decrees. Yet today by and large it is abandoned, and that abandonment
leaves the documents and decrees that relied on it almost mute and ineffectual." And

and practices of others? How are we to relate to other people of faith who, everywhere they are encountered and known, live lives as deep or sometimes deeper than practitioners of our home tradition? And how, in our commitment to tolerance, can we go beyond the inclusivist approach, recognizing and respecting the validity of many different religious traditions without undermining the accepted truths of our own religion?

The catch is that, in opening ourselves to the panoply of other religions, all manner of questions will arise: Is Jesus really the incarnated son of God? Is he the one and only path? Does the uniqueness of Christ in human history mean that Christians are special?[24] Better or more blessed than others? What does incarnation mean? Is the Hindu god Krishna, too, an incarnation? Was the Buddha Śākyamuni truly awakened? Does awakening as presented in the Buddhist scriptures occur for non-Buddhists? Does it really occur for Buddhist practitioners?[25] Why is Muhammad, caught in his seventh-century time frame, the greatest of all the prophets? Why does revelation end at any one time? Or does it?

These are important questions, not least because they highlight critical issues about central doctrines within the traditions, doctrines that orient us within the near neighborhood of the everyday practice of faith. Pluralist models of theology tend to engender anxiety among the faithful about the very nature of such doctrines and traditions, raising questions about the languages in which faith is expressed and presented and the cultural conventions that nourish the practice of that faith. These critical issues of language and doctrine turn us back to look at all specific religious teachings, calling them into ever-deepening question and demanding an ever-broader apologetic—an apologetic not only for this or that faith, but for the validity of *any* faith that would claim truth,[26] and for faith language and creedal affirmation in general.

---

again 32: "A theology is the product not only of a faith but also of a culture. It is cultural change that had made Scholasticism no longer relevant and demands the development of new theological method and style, continuous indeed with the old, yet meeting all the genuine exigencies both of the Christian religion and of up-to-date philosophy, science, and scholarship."

24. See Williams, "Finality of Jesus Christ," 93–106, who rejects the tripartite set of options of exclusivism, inclusivism, and pluralism, for a more nuanced and historically grounded witness to Christ. We are not about "winning arguments for once and all."

25. For critical reflection, see the essays in Jackson and Makransky, *Buddhist Theology.*

26. These issues are clearly identified and described by then Cardinal Ratzinger (Pope

Religious thinkers who would recommend the pluralist attitude toward other religions, recognizing many equally valid paths, nevertheless still need to develop an accompanying apologetic for their particular faith affirmation and creed. It is not enough to assert the full and rich validity of many different faith traditions without at the same time offering a cogent recommendation for following a particular tradition—unless the point is precisely *not* to follow any one tradition. And then that universalist creed itself stands in need of some justification.

The issues of doctrine and language that are raised in the pluralist discussion are tied inextricably to the many assertions that are customarily made within a given faith tradition—on matters of faith and reason, of identity and difference, of God and reality, of salvation and damnation, of truth and revelation. Indeed, what about revelation? What about scripture? If all questions can be swiftly answered and any issues resolved by rapid appeal to scripture, then the entire interfaith endeavor collapses on the ruins of some fundamentalism or other. Tolerance counts in that case only when scripture says that it does. How then are we to understand our own scriptures? This last question needs to be addressed first and foremost, for it preconditions all the others.

Whose revelation? Whose scripture?

Every major religious tradition proclaims a truth from beyond human knowing—revealed by God, flowing from the ultimate realm, or heard from the beginning, and encapsulated somehow in sacred texts. Those who have attempted to go outside the scriptures of their own tradition to consider alien traditions in depth, reading their texts as possibly relevant to faith experience, are often criticized by their co-religionists. Their study of others' sacred texts is seen as a defect in their adherence to their own faith, in that they are departing—or so it would appear—from the truly revealed word. In this case, revealed scripture not only serves as a source of truth for a given tradition but may also act to constrict the spirit, to place an obstacle in the way of interfaith understanding. Indeed, some would argue that interfaith discussion should be avoided altogether, based as it is on assumptions and preconditions that already, before a word is uttered, lead one away from committed faith.[27]

Benedict XVI), in his book *Truth and Tolerance*, 115–137.

27. Griffiths, "Interreligious Polemics," 32.

It is true that theological positions expressed in the sacred writings of one religious tradition often do explicitly negate the teachings of a different tradition. What is affirmed in one tradition does sometimes preclude options in another. Assuredly and patently, all religions are not saying the same thing, and what one says is not always congruent with what another says. The confident—and not uncommon—assumption of some open-minded persons that there is a basic, sometimes one-to-one, correspondence and complementarity between the revealed scriptures of all major faith traditions can actually become an obstacle to interreligious understanding. Minds and hearts are not opened by quick and easy conclusions that level differences by simply bludgeoning them from view and negating the particularity of each faith as expressed in its sacred texts.

Thus, a crucial first question for people of faith becomes: How can we approach other religions and their sacred writings intelligently and openly without denigrating the truth of our own scriptures? How can we do this without undermining that foundational theology that derives from revelation and scripture, the warrants of authentic faith?

Sacred scripture does indeed serve as the authority for most of the world's major religious traditions. However, as we will discuss more fully below, scripture is by no means a clear and unambiguous guide on all issues, for the simple reason that all scriptures are tied to their particular human histories. All are accepted as inspired indeed, but all were written at specific points in history in specific languages for specific doctrinal purposes and with specific readers and hearers in mind. They taste of their original, on-the-ground cultural milieu, so the guidance that they offer is often oblique and needs to be drawn out by interpretation in light of new times and new life situations. Even those scriptures whose meaning appears to be the most obvious and explicit need to be interpreted, for we must understand just what they are being obvious and explicit about.[28] Moreover, the understanding of scripture grows over time, as new insights are drawn from ancient witnesses and further implications are evolved to answer new situations.[29]

---

28. As expressed in the title of the basic scripture of Yogācāra Buddhism, *The Scripture on the Explication of Underlying Meaning (Samdhinirmocana-sūtra)*.

29. See Asaṅga's *Great Vehicle*, 54–55, which teaches that interpretation of scriptures "consists in explaining and analyzing texts that have been previously taught [by Buddha as scripture] in the light of later commentaries."

In Christian theology, the nature of revelation and scripture can be understood in the same manner that the early creeds explained the nature of Christ. The scriptures are the word of God, and that very word becomes incarnate in Christ. If Christ be truly and fully both divine and human, so likewise is the revealed truth of the Bible fully and completely both the word of *God* and the *word* of God. It is revelatory of what lies beyond, but at the same time it is truly and fully a construct of human language and culture—as is every word and every language.

To regard scriptural language as entirely apart and different from the conventional language of the world is the same as maintaining that Jesus was only divine—that despite his human appearance, he was not fully incarnated as human with a body and soul and all those physiological and emotional characteristics that describe us as humans, that he only *masqueraded* as a man. The early councils of the Church refuted this claim as the "docetic" heresy. Its analogue in regard to scripture is likewise to be rejected as a denial of the economy of the incarnation. Revealed scripture is incarnated in culture, and its language neither negates nor usurps ordinary human language and conventional grammar. Even revelation from God must follow the rules of grammar! Furthermore, revelations must be congruent with cultural norms and expectations, and still value the revealed words as both divinely inspired and humanly constructed. If we do otherwise in insistence on wooden, fundamentalistic readings, we commit the heresy of a docetic hermeneutics, in which scriptural words are not really human words at all, but purely divine terms that just pretend to be human.

Our response to the scriptures of our tradition is properly not to employ them as excuses to whine plaintively about the ills of modern culture nor to proffer them as proof that our personal theological opinions are correct. Rather, we are to regard scripture as a guide to authentic practice that embodies and embraces the truths expressed in scripture and realizes them in actual living. *The Letter of James* in the New Testament directs attention to scripture, but it also teaches that true religion consists in visiting widows and orphans:

> If any one thinks he is religious and does not bridle his tongue but deceives his heart, this man's religion is vain. Religion that is pure and undefiled before God and the Father is this: to visit orphans and widows in their affliction, and to keep oneself unstained from the world (1:26–27).

This passage from James's letter is the only place in the entire Bible where the term "religion" is mentioned, and the statement seems intended to undermine the notion that "pure" religion is either cultic practice or doctrinal stance. That kind of religion, James is saying, is empty of meaning and vain, no matter how correct it may be. Indeed, doctrinal religion does not figure significantly at all in James's message. He insists that no theory can substitute for engaged practice, which is to be directed toward "orphans and widows," those without protection or support, the most vulnerable members of the community. Faith, responding to scriptural revelation, must be incarnated in actual languages, cultures, and lives.

But false religion for James is not simply the failure to practice authentically, neglecting to visit the poor and the marginal. False religion is also vacillating in doubt and discrimination, focusing on human measures of reality, on human judgments rather than on Torah. Faith is made genuine by engagement in works of justice and peace, but faith is more than that: It demands a docile, unbiased but critical, acceptance of the teachings of the tradition, a tradition that is grounded on warranted scripture.

In our time, many find themselves unable to affirm the scriptures of any faith tradition. Some remain under the influence of the modern culture of the Enlightenment, which taught us to put our trust in empirical evidence, intelligence, and reason.[30] They demand more "objective" proof than the scriptures offer, and they regard the very notion of sacred writings as culturally naïve. Others are more affected by postmodern viewpoints, however innocently, and regard so-called objectivity and reason as mere cultural constructs. They characterize the sacred writings of all traditions as culturally biased and arrogant.

That part of contemporary culture that regards itself as open-minded, fair, and progressive demands tolerance toward competing truth claims and requires us to reject anything that would present itself as the one and only truth. In practice, this all-enveloping tolerance is not often articulated; indeed, among Western intellectuals it is simply assumed. Its opposite is regarded as in some sense "fundamentalist" and is thus filtered out of the visible intellectual spectrum. Many conservative religionists of course maintain with increasing and bulldogged insistence the absolute and literal truth of their tradition's holy writ, but broad segments of soci-

---

30. See Ratzinger, *Truth and Tolerance*, 115–21.

ety dismiss just as bull-doggedly not only the truth of scripture but also organized religion in general as simply irrelevant. Indeed, in this moment of world history, the more fundamentalist preachers appear on television, the more people reject Christian practice, for such an approach demands simple adherence to the literal word of the preacher. Sadly, a year or so ago, we here in the United States saw a fundamentalist preacher, Pat Robertson, recommend on the air the murder of the head of state of another country, because he did not like his politics.

But, despite repeated declarations of their imminent demise (Freud, Marx, some of my neighbors), religious traditions do perdure. So, as tempting as it may be to walk away from all the questions, there is no easy way out: Is the Bible the true scripture? The Hebrew Bible alone? The New Testament? The *Bhagavadgita*? The *Lotus Scripture*? The *Perfection of Wisdom Scriptures* of Mahāyāna Buddhism? Or the *Qur'an*? If we are not to sweep all sacred writ into the dustbin of historical irrelevancy, how do we choose? Who gets to judge *which* scripture is true scripture? Can they all be true? Is all of this merely today's Zen kōan?[31]

How can we take any scripture seriously and still move beyond a situation of dueling fundamentalisms, of competing sacred texts, each identified with some monocultural and normative theology, each rejecting every other religious tradition either with supercilious disdain or with compassionate regret? How can we have confidence in the authority of a religion's teaching that warrants its own status as true? And yet, if we acknowledge our cultural limitations and the cultural boundedness of our faith tradition, are we not thereby rendered incapable of making any faith commitment at all? Is a faith commitment itself necessarily a sign of culturally narrow-minded jingoism?

Pluralism: the picture gallery

Certainly there are problems with the exclusive stance—the insistence that one religious faith, validated by its own revelation or tradition, already possesses the true picture in light of which all other religions are simply untrue and to be excluded from serious consideration. Such exclusive views, especially those that claim a linear revelation from God to

---

31. Actually, this option attracts me, for to the question of which is the true religion; the Master could merely mumble "*Yu* (yes)." Or perhaps the more traditional "*Mu* (nah)."

our very own ancestors in the faith are culturally dissonant. They have been excoriated easily and repeatedly by many a theological study, and their distorted, narrow practices are dramatized in novels and movies about closed-minded missionaries.[32] The commonsense spirituality of our twenty-first century urges upon us the awareness that this approach cannot be right.

But there are problems with the inclusive stance as well, for it still maintains that one's own faith possesses the complete picture, warranted by its scripture and tradition, in terms of which the faiths of others are less complete, even if perhaps expectantly valid in view of their prospective growth. Buddhists, in this view, may be regarded as "hidden" Christians. Alternatively, a Buddhist may conclude that people who are comforted by Christian practice in this lifetime will, because of their good karmic actions, be reborn hereafter into a more fortuitous situation and realize the awakening of a buddha.

Inclusive thinkers, who grade other religious traditions as sharing partially in the truth of their own, do take a step toward affirming the validity of those traditions. Although other faiths might be a grade lower, at least they are in the same classroom. But to evaluate other faiths in terms of one's own grants them validity only by a self-referencing double-back. Such an inclusive strategy suffers from an unavoidable but culturally inappropriate sense of superiority. Far better to preach one's own faith unabashedly than to claim that it validates someone else's faith.

These attitudes—the assurance that one's own faith has either the "true picture" or the "complete picture"—occur in many different places, not only in the West. The Eurocentrism that conceived the rest of the world as inferior is matched by the Chinese conceit of being "the Central Kingdom." It is paralleled by Indian practices of seeing all foreign traditions as lesser attempts to express truths long known to the seers of the Vedas and the Upanishads.[33] It appears in Muslim notions that Islam is the final revelation and in Japanese notions that Zen is the true heart of all true practice.[34]

32. Examples are James Michener's *Hawaii*, Peter Matthiessen's *At Play in the Fields of the Lord*, Barbara Kingsolver's *The Poisonwood Bible*, Brian Moore's *Black Robe*, and the Roland Joffé film *Mission*.

33. Radhakrishnan, "Indian Approach to the Religious Problem," 178–79, on "religion as experience."

34. See Suzuki, *Essays in Zen Buddhism*, his famous debate with the humanist and

Recognizing the inadequacy of both the exclusivist and inclusivist stances, many broad-minded people today favor instead the bolder stance of pluralism. They acknowledge many religious traditions as valid and effective, and they appreciate them as offering authentic pictures of the real—rather like the way we used to enjoy viewing the slides our friends and neighbors brought home from their tourist travels to foreign realms. At the same time, they recognize that all religions are imperfect, language–bound embodiments of the full truth. Pluralists confess the beauty, truth, and salvific efficacy of the many world religious traditions while maintaining that no one tradition has the one "true picture" or even the "complete picture." Rather, they aver, we all have a valid picture—and we can visit the world's "picture gallery" of faiths and view an impartial and pleasing display of all the traditions. And so these three options abide: the one true picture, the complete picture, and the picture gallery. And to the pluralist, who can always go home to practice, the last of these is indeed the greatest.

The pluralist stance harmonizes well with our new common awareness of the multiplicity of faith traditions and of how deeply those traditions are embedded within their respective cultures. This stance is liberal and it is open-minded. It is also much to educated taste, for it allows one to maintain a sense of religious faith as a personal choice that is not really subject to public adjudication.[35] *De fidei gustibus non est disputandum!* In matters of personal preference—whether gustatory or religious—one should not judge others. Our culture accepts that religion is a matter of individual choice, not unlike an ultimate form of selecting a dinner entrée from the restaurant menu.[36] Better to assume that—whatever the religious label—we are all actually worshiping the same God, or the same Reality, than to indulge in the fundamentalisms of the intransigent. There

critical textual scholar Hu Shih, who argued in his "Ch'an (Zen) Buddhism in China: Its History and Method," that Zen is one historical movement among others. Suzuki argued in his "Zen: A Reply to Hu Shih," that Zen is ahistorical, the dynamic heart of all religious practice. For a critique of centrist Buddhism, see Hakamaya, *Hongaku shisō hihan* [Critiques of the Doctrine of Original Enlightenment] and *Hihan bukkyō* [Critical Buddhism], and, in English, the essays on Critical Buddhism in Hubbard and Swanson, *Pruning the Bodhi Tree.*

35. The classic statement of this cultural shift is Herberg's *Protestant, Catholic, Jew,* which treats the move away from public religious intensity to a doctrinally gentler, less doctrinally insistent citizenship.

36. Griffiths, *Problems of Religious Diversity,* 5.

are many distinct paths to the ultimate, and in the pluralist view the paths of all the major traditions are adequate and equal.[37]

It is only within the last century that an explicit philosophy of pluralism has come to be seen as a possible theological stance, and already that pluralistic view has become the broadly accepted commonsense spirituality of our age, defining the tolerance that lies at the base of our cultural norms. Modern educated culture around the globe is marked by a professed tolerance for and commitment to the differences among people, no matter how much this modern culture might fail in constructing conditions that enable people to be truly different.

A prime mover impelling us in the pluralist direction is our keen attunement to the sad history of ethnic and religious warfare—the reality that people have killed and continue to kill one another in the name of religious belief. We know in our common cultural hearts that such barbarities must cease, that narrow-minded arrogance must be recognized as an error and a sin of our past, that such actions have no part in interfaith relations.

And yet we know full well that religious delusions reappear, rising out of the past again and again to give license once more to barbarous behavior. This knowledge tempts us to conclude that strong religious identities, rather than propelling people toward compassionate practice, tend instead to freeze people in self-enclosed bastions of fearful insecurity and potential violence. So entrenched are the religious conflicts in some places that this story is told of a British official appointed to Northern Ireland: Upon arrival, he is asked, "Are you Protestant or Catholic?" Wisely avoiding either alternative, he identifies himself as an atheist. But the issue will not go away, for (perhaps with a nod to James Joyce) he is next asked, "Well, yes, but are you a Protestant atheist or a Catholic atheist?"

In the face of such realities, the pluralist stance has become a very popular view among most educated Christians, not only Unitarian Universalists, and it is certainly not an unreasonable one. The pluralist view can also be supported by the many Mahāyāna Buddhist texts that characterize many teachings as skillful means. As noted in the discussion on inclusivism, this notion can be used to account for inferior paths devised for the less adept, but it may also refer to any religious teaching, even to Buddhism itself. In this view, the truth is never articulated in any language, never able to be drawn out at all, for it remains beyond human

37. See Hick, *Interpretation of Religion*, and Knitter, *Jesus and the Other Names*, and *One Earth, Many Religions*.

thought and image, in the silence of a master like Vimalakīrti, beyond even the Buddha Śākyamuni himself.[38]

Many pluralists believe that truth may be experienced only mystically through religious experience and can never be captured in words or doctrines. This kind of mystic orientation, it is claimed by many,[39] is found in every religious tradition, and some would identify it as the single, common source for those traditions. In the Zen taught by D.T. Suzuki, it is the silent experience beyond all words that constitutes the root awakening of Zen and is the heart of all religion.[40] All religions in their heart of hearts, it is maintained, come together in the one mystical experience beyond all doctrine and all image.

A refusal to be bounded by any tradition or any faith is a most attractive option to sophisticated minds. It liberates one not only from the temptation of intolerant arrogance, but also from the narrow confines of self-validating definitions. It moves one toward Nietzsche's frightening but invigorating freedom to conduct experiments with truth, to create value in non-sectarian authenticity. Even Dietrich Bonhoeffer, pious man that he was, speaks in his *Letters From Prison* of a courageous "religionless" Christianity. Our modern aversion to identifying with religious traditions derives not only from our familiarity with religious bias and violence, but also from a desire not to be fenced into our own small corner of the world. After all, it is held, we are all in this life together, and perhaps we should recognize that all of us are engaged in the spiritual quest for a silent and all-encompassing fullness.

Contributing to the contemporary distaste for narrow religious views, Nietzsche, Marx, Derrida, and a host of other modern and postmodern philosophers have made us acutely aware of the formative influence of language and culture upon religious belief. Because of our particular histories and specific identities, forged always within particular cultures and languages, it is not by accident that Christians rarely think to meditate upon the eternal Buddha of the *Lotus Scripture*, or that Buddhists hardly ever speak of union with Jesus. Pluralists, aware of the diversity of cultures and languages, argue that each tradition is valid and appropriate in its context. A religious tradition, rather like a language, as George

38. Nagao, "Silence of the Buddha," 40–41.

39. See, for example, Stace, *Mysticism and Philosophy*, 31–38.

40. See Keenan, "Limits of Thomas Merton's Understanding of Buddhism," 118–33.

A. Lindbeck contends, follows its own grammar and constructs its own world of meaning.[41]

The courageous Buddhist monk and prolific author Thich Nhat Hanh, in his book *Going Home: Jesus and Buddha as Brothers*, presents a common basis for everything a Buddhist might experience in analogous Christian mystical experience.[42] He has by force of history and choice of openness, engaged deeply in interfaith dialogue and practice. Emphasizing the commonalties between Christianity and Buddhism, he goes so far as to claim that any differences between the two are superficial, a matter of degree rather than a question of core truth claims. Thich Nhat Hanh argues—quietly and gently, to be sure—that truth lies at the center, with multiple paths leading to it, and that multiple traditions may complement one another within a single practitioner.

Thich Nhat Hanh's views take on more nuance with his dismissal of some particular religious beliefs; he discards even some notions found in Buddhism, such as the heaven of the Pure Land school. Though he does not accept all religious claims as valid, he does extend his pluralistic acceptance to Christianity without reservation. No Christian can read him without appreciation. Strangely, while many Christians would hesitate to teach their own doctrine in an interfaith context for fear of offending, this Zen Buddhist monk champions Christian doctrine as an alternate path to the same truth that he has long tasted and taught.

Thich Nhat Hanh sketches out the basic similarities he sees between Buddhism and Christianity: God and nirvāna, the Buddha and Christ, the Kingdom of God and enlightenment, the Five Precepts and the Nicene Creed, Dharma and the teachings of Jesus. Although differences certainly exist, he maintains that most are issues of degree rather than of substance, or are insignificant technicalities. For example, he resolves the apparent conflict between Buddhist emptiness and the Christian God's substantive existence by claiming that God is separate from the level of existence on which we experience all things, and thus there can be nothingness and God simultaneously. And, he says, for all practical purposes reincarnation and no-self are obstacles that a Christian practitioner can ignore. Thich Nhat Hanh posits no absolute truth, placing the emphasis instead upon

---

41. Lindbeck, *Nature of Doctrine*, 31–40, 79–84, and throughout the book.
42. Thich Nhat Hanh, *Going Home*, 135–43 and 171–202.

living in the present moment with an eye for experience and insight. This, of course, is bewitchingly attractive.

The trouble with pluralism

Still, one can only visit a picture gallery; one cannot comfortably live there. We might pledge ourselves to a particular picture of reality, but no one commits to a gallery. Quite the contrary, it is simply impossible to view and appreciate all the pictures in a gallery, for they are many. Once a large van Gogh exhibition came to the Philadelphia Museum of Art, and I hurried down to see some of my favorite works. Alas, the number of van Gogh aficionados in that city was so great that all had to move along quickly past each painting without lingering. What a waste of time that was! Years later, I had an opportunity to visit the van Gogh Museum in Amsterdam one quiet Sunday morning. There, I was able to stand before "The Crows" for perhaps an hour—indeed, so engrossed was I that I do not remember how long I gazed at that painting. It is burnt into my mind now, for I kept returning to look again and deeper: the thickness of the crow paint, the V-shaped dirt road leading away from the hay-like fields, and the sea-like clouds that hover darkly over the lighter water/sky. The more I looked, the more I saw. The more I saw, the more I treasured Vincent van Gogh's ability to execute such a work. There were many other paintings in that Amsterdam museum, but I was unable to take them in that day. In a sense, I feel that this experience illustrates Karl Rahner's contention: "It is only possible to live, religiously speaking, in absolute affirmation."[43] And that affirmation must be grounded in a particular vernacular tradition. A picture gallery of religious options will not suffice, much less a museum.

Even in Zen, wherein religious language is never itself absolute but rather just a finger pointing to the moon of awakening, that language must point correctly. For many people, faith is a matter of full and complete, indeed absolute, commitment; only that can truly satisfy the deepest needs of the human heart. Even if it is a myth that carries the power of religious transformation, that myth must symbolize and enflesh something that is itself quite real in order to be meaningful and efficacious.

"Once told, that is, revealed, a myth becomes apodictic truth; it establishes a truth which is absolute. . . . It is this reason that myth is bound

---

43. Rahner, *Sacramentum Mundi*, 1:302.

up with ontology; it speaks only of *realities*, of what *really* happened."[44] Religious truth must do more than simply assert a view of the world; its goal is to transform the practitioner and to redirect this person's life.[45] And the power of a tradition to convert and transform depends upon its having convincing meaning and impelling force within a particular cultural milieu at a specific point in time. Such transformative power must be grounded in an affirmation of abiding and determinative validity.

Herein lies the problem with pluralism, for it seems to undermine any such absolute affirmation, as well as any commitment to practice that might follow in its train. Because of the pervasive influence of the pluralist stance in recent years, it has become academically suspect to argue for the truth of any one religious tradition over others, and so a loose and amorphous ecumenism has become the common paradigm for dialogue between the world's faiths.

Certainly the history of colonialism offers evidence aplenty to discredit the practice of imposing one's own religious truth on others who are not necessarily seeking it. Academics are rightly wary of introducing missionary implications into their studies on religion. As an alternative, they do generic studies of faith as symbol structure, or of religion in the context of the history of ideas, with a polite nod or two toward Gandhi and his very Indian inclusivism of many religions at once.[46]

Rather than to be seen as an apologist for one faith, in academia it is safer by far to support a pluralist philosophy of religions that understands religious experience as mystical, and links mystic awareness to a gentle respect for, and affirmation of, other traditions. Mystical experiences themselves are distinguished from the specific linguistic and dogmatic formulations in which they are expressed. In such a unitive vision of the sum of all our hopes, all differences tend to fade to black, to that dark night in which one may come into contact with the God who cannot be seen, to the awakening that cannot be earned or described.

Blurring the differences does ease the conversation between different faiths, as demonstrated in the work of Thich Nhat Hanh. A wise and tested Zen monk formed in the crucible of the war in Vietnam, he reached together with American anti-war protestors toward a peace that could

44. Eliade, *Sacred and the Profane*, 95.

45. Streng, *Emptiness*, 17–18, and *Ways of Being Religious*, 6.

46. See Martel, *Life of Pi*, 82, wherein Pi Patel "attracts religions the way a dog attracts fleas."

encompass us all. I admire his courage and am always moved by his writings.[47] Still, I demur, for I do not think that Thich Nhat Hanh's pluralist approach is an adequate response to the important question: How can we be radically open to other religions and still entrust ourselves fully to a particular faith and practice?

As religious beings, simply learning to be open-minded and unbiased does not satisfy our heart's desire. We desire to be one with God, to be awakened with the Buddha, to submit ourselves entirely to the will of Allah. But wanting to do all these things, how can we do any? If we mix or reduce or blend or pick and choose, we seem at some point or another to do violence both to the vernacular tradition of our native faith and to the vernacular traditions of other peoples' faiths—and all for the sake of a globalized, homogenized overview of wisdom or religious experience.

As the saying goes, the most open-minded of persons is the one without a brain.

The oft-quoted Indian tale about the blind men and the elephant is frequently used to illustrate the limits of human language and experience and thereby to demonstrate the need for a pluralist philosophy of religions. A group of blind men are trying to identify the object—an elephant—that stands unseen before them. One bumps into the elephant's solid side and concludes that it is surely a wall. Another grasps hold of its broad flat ear and concludes that it is a palm leaf. Yet a third clutches its tail and thinks he has a snake. A fourth feels around one leg and identifies it as a pillar, while a fifth is sure the trunk is a hose. We are all blind men groping in the dark, each feebly attempting to give an adequate account of our experience.

The parable is a good one, but it fails to acknowledge that there is another participant in this story—the sighted narrator who alone can see what it is that everyone else is trying to figure out. This observer knows that it is an elephant, while all the religiously blind men, try as they might, cannot describe the creature adequately because each experiences it only in part. But who in our religious world ever gets to be the detached, see-it-all observer? From what lofty vantage point can anyone see the reality that defies all the vain attempts of us poor sightless creatures below?

---

47. He calls to mind for me apophatic writers like Church Fathers Gregory of Nyssa and Dionysius—who actually did write mystical theology—and modern writers like Thomas Merton and Alan Jones. But their writings are meant for those inside the tradition, to deepen an already practiced faith.

The very force of critical philosophy in the last half century would disallow the meta-position of this observer who has such a language- and culture-free viewpoint. We can all of course ride in airplanes and look down upon the weary world below. But even high over the earth, the announcements are invariably made in the languages used on that same earth. There is no meta-position that transcends us all, and no meta-language in which to articulate religious truth.

Many who enunciate the pluralist position are well aware of the potentially relativistic and meaning-negating discourse of this interfaith philosophy. They strive consequently to eschew a naïve relativism that does not seem quite adequate to them. As Diana Eck explains, " ... [P]luralism is not simply relativism. It does not displace or eliminate deep religious commitments or secular commitments for that matter. It is, rather, the encounter of commitments."[48] Eck's non-relativistic pluralism would avoid the typical inclusivist tolerance toward other traditions as genetically lower stages of one's own true faith, and embrace the other with the expectation of finding value beyond that which is present within the home religion.

Still, the pluralism that claims not to be relativistic lives in dialectic tension with most other versions of pluralism, and it lacks cogent argumentation. It is more the statement of a cherished goal, or perhaps the description of an authentic practice, than a philosophy of religions.

48. Eck, *New Religious America*, 71.

2

Toward a Workable Philosophy of Religions

If not pluralism, what?

WE HAVE REJECTED THE exclusivist stance with its summary dismissal of all faiths other than one's own. We have considered inclusivism, which usually evolves from within one particular theological understanding. Although some forms of inclusivism articulated today do strive for a radical opening to other traditions while being grounded within their own,[1] they have not explicated much of a philosophy for being so grounded. We have also noted the pitfalls of pluralism, which slides all too easily toward relativism and a consequent weakening of faith commitment.

The open-mindedness of pluralism would seem much to be preferred to the alternatives. But how can pluralism avoid the charge that it reduces the faith claims of all traditions to mere cultural artifacts, and in practice almost inevitably—although against all the theologically-nuanced intentions of its best proponents—leads people to regard all religions as equally insignificant mush?

Pluralism can indeed set people free from the confines of an enmeshing culture, liberating them from the constraints of classical absolutes. Thus freed, they may then sample a little of this and a little of that from the newly opened "divine deli" of this pluralist world.[2] A little of this and a little of that from the smorgasbord of faiths, though, is not in

---

1. So I find the works of Francis X. Clooney and James L. Fredericks richly suggestive and fully textured, precisely because they lack any overarching plan or ideology of how to adjudicate among the faiths; rather, they are intentionally patient and thus hesitant to adopt such an ideological norm. Also I have found very helpful indeed the philosophical theology of O'Leary, in his *Questioning Back* and *Religious Pluralism and Christian Truth*.

2. As described and critiqued by Berthrong, *Divine Deli*.

the end a soul-satisfying position. It is but one stage in what at best may become an ever-expanding awareness of other people's faiths—and eventually perhaps, a deeper insight into one's own tradition. Or the divine deli may merely deliver a goulash of religious traditions, a mishmash that robs each of its taste and meaning. When all is said that we can now say, people may well conclude, it really does not matter which faith language one speaks.

What then is an appropriate attitude toward the variety of religions in the world? What contours would an adequate philosophy of religions take?

It is clear to me that this dilemma cannot be solved, or even addressed, from within a single culture or theological tradition. All too many theologians and religious leaders are willing to pronounce judgment on others' faith traditions when all they know of those traditions is what some of their co-religionists have written on the subject. Their monocultural point of view leaves them ill-informed and ill-equipped to say anything convincing about other traditions, or even to dialogue with them. Very commonly, the theologians of any one faith lack experience of sustained and direct contact with adherents of other faiths and moreover have had little or no exposure to the primary sources, the scriptures and texts, of those faiths.

Not only is it difficult for trained theologians to extricate themselves from their monocultural context in order to approach the richness of other faiths, but a certain sense of insular defensiveness would seem to incline them toward avoidance of such encounters. But the very intractability of this situation signals its importance.

A satisfactory approach to this situation must first and foremost be appropriate to the actual traditions of Jews, Christians, Buddhists, Hindus, Muslims, and Taoists. It must skillfully respect and philosophically account for the faith and practice of the many religious traditions as they exist. This means that it would have to pay close attention to what these traditions actually do teach, considering not only this or that text or this or that teacher, but that tradition's dynamic and ongoing development over time.

Both Buddhist critiques of Christians as making supernatural claims that pander to the weak and Christian attacks on Buddhists as otherworldly escapists are caricatures. These distorting characterizations permit each to dismiss the other's tradition.[3] We must go beyond such distortions. Not that there do not exist in every tradition texts and teachers that can be faulted. There are weak and needy Christians seeking comfort, and there are Buddhist escapists. Indeed, one can even find instances of Buddhist god-attachment—a Chinese proverb from Taiwan speaks of "clinging to the feet of Buddha the day before the exam"—and Christian versions of aloof and escapist other-worldliness.

The deeper one goes into the study of any tradition, the more complex the questions become. Soon one realizes that each tradition draws on its own resources to address its own weaknesses, and can hardly be dismissed as unaware of the problems of delusion and false attachment. Pope John Paul II criticized Buddhism for being otherworldly,[4] and indeed some of the earliest scriptures are so. But Buddhist thinkers themselves have been acutely aware of that very issue and have dealt with it in variously creative ways designed to draw the practitioner toward awakened engagement in this world of our human endeavor.

Similarly, in their insistence upon the supernatural person and role of Christ, Christians appear to Jews and Muslims to fail to appreciate the oneness of God. But, well aware of the implications of their faith in Christ, the early Fathers of the Church enunciated the doctrine of the Trinity expressly to negate the supernatural imagination that would see Christ as another god beside God.[5] The point here is that any philosophy of religions has to be able to respect and listen to, study and understand, and track and follow, the ongoing teachings of the various faith traditions. It will not suffice to rely upon some colleague who professes an acquaintance with world religions to brief one adequately on what those other people think and believe.

Second and equally important, our approach to the religious traditions ought to be primarily philosophical, not theological. Within any

3. For example, Chödrön, *When Things Fall Apart*, 39; and the March 20, 1997 interview of then Cardinal Ratzinger by the French magazine *L'Exprese*. See Allen, *Pope Benedict XVI*, 253. I think it proper to distinguish between what Joseph Ratzinger said as the Prefect of the Congregation for the Doctrine of the Faith when a Cardinal, and what he says as Pope, as he himself has remarked. They are different tasks and call forth different gifts.

4. John Paul II, *Crossing the Threshold of Hope*, 85–90.

5. Pelikan, *Christian Tradition*, 1:132. On the dismissive attitude of Christians toward emerging Islam and its rejection of Trinity, see Daniel, *Islam and the West*, 208–09; also Hoyland, *Seeing Islam*, 1–52, and throughout his presentation of primary sources.

one tradition, a theological approach is indeed appropriate, inasmuch as it may both remain faithful to its tradition and lead its adherents toward open and insightful engagement with others. But in interfaith dialogue, no single tradition or its theology can claim the privilege of providing a grid whereby others are to be viewed or judged. If one first has to take refuge in the Three Jewels of Buddhism, then all non-Buddhists will be excluded from the understanding sketched by that approach. It may indeed enhance the faith of Christians to regard others as embraced within the Fatherhood of God, but such a theology appeals only to the already thus theologized.

Nor will an approach that simply sweeps aside all differences suffice. When that modern Indian statesman and sage S. Radhakrishnan writes that "there is no reason to believe that there are fundamental differences between the east and west,"[6] one rightly detects an intuitional pluralism at work. There is little point in writing or arguing a purely pluralist philosophy of religions that in the end asserts that everything is, in its own way, correct.[7] This is to devalue each distinct religion by reducing all actual, on-the-ground teachings, claims, and faith-philosophies to epiphenomena of something that a given pluralist thinker considers to be the genuine, universally shared truth. At the very least, to do so is again to invite the all-too-common conclusion that "anything goes."

The philosophy of religions that we seek must ground practitioners within their traditions in all their differences, with full fervor and vigorous intellectual commitment and—at the same time and by the same token—open those very practitioners to other traditions so that we might enrich one another, learn to respect and cherish one another, and live peacefully in the world of our common concern.[8] The philosophy we seek thus must be able to explicate the significance of religious language itself within the various traditions. Tied tightly to the doctrines expressed, our philosophy of religions should both defend the many doctrines (or rather allow others committed to these doctrines to defend them) and also of-

6. Radhakrishnan, "Indian Approach to the Religious Problem," 173.

7. But see Martel, *Life of Pi*, 70: "I can well imagine an atheist's last words: 'White, white! L-L-Love! My God'—and the deathbed leap of faith. Whereas the agnostic, if he stays true to his reasonable self, if he stays beholden to dry, yeastless factuality, might try to explain the warm light bathing him by saying, 'Possibly a f-f-falling oxygenation of the b-b-brain,' and so, to the very end, lack imagination and miss the better story."

8. Confer and compare: Knitter, *One Earth, Many Religions*.

fer a philosophic apologetic for the truth-expressing words and creeds of each religion. Both the openness of tolerance and the defense of faith have to be embraced in an adequate account of religious pluralism.

Going to ground and learning the vernacular

A theological Esperanto will not suffice for our task. Esperanto has never caught on precisely because it is not the mother tongue of any group of real people in any living culture. Each vernacular faith tradition has its own vernacular, its own mother tongue, in both a linguistic and a cultural sense. A tradition may over time move across a language or cultural boundary, but in order to thrive in new terrain it will renew its vernacular as it becomes encultured, or en-earthed in that place.[9]

Each and every participant in interfaith dialogue has roots in some vernacular faith culture. And each faith culture speaks in a specific language or set of languages. The classical languages of Buddhism are Sanskrit and Chinese, not Greek or Latin; its modern languages are primarily Southeast or East Asian, not primarily European. Arabic and Persian are central to the study of Islam, not Japanese or Korean. In order to truly engage and come to terms with traditions that are alien and unfamiliar to us, we must learn their vernaculars. We need to do this for the simple reason that, having moved next door, they impinge upon our theologies and our apologetics. And while we strive to understand the roots and vernaculars of alien traditions, we must also develop a deeper awareness of the cultural and historical construction of our own native faith. "[W]here commitments are explicitly at issue, it is just as well to pay attention from the start to the particular ways in which one's interests and narrowed concerns affect one's work."[10] Without being grounded in one's own tradition, one can never reach the ground of another.

Both Pope Benedict and the Dalai Lama warn against leaping across the wide divides between the traditions so that we end up floating in mid-air betwixt and between, with our feet planted nowhere. Attentive to the plain fact that every faith tradition stands at the heart of its own culture,[11] we must assiduously study the actual teachings both of our own tradition

9. Schachter-Shalomi, "Interview," 87–89. Also note Keenan, *How Master Mou Removes Our Doubts*, which treats the enculturation of Buddhism in China.

10. Clooney, "Seeing Through Texts," 42.

11. Ratzinger, *Truth and Tolerance*, 71.

and of the other. Further, we will need to listen to critiques and be open to rethinking, radical rethinking. There is no way to sensitively approach and understand other peoples' faiths without forging an opening within one's own faith. When no single culture can set norms for the world, no monocultural norm of reality will avail for the tasks ahead. Excluded are both classical norms—which in the past differentiated our culture from error—and universalistic norms that would cut off the limbs of all faith traditions in order to fit them all into the same-sized bed.

It is clear that none who would think on faith today, however much they would like to do so, can live entirely isolated within the bounds of a single vernacular culture or vernacular religious tradition. But this does not mean that we cannot live within our traditions, as vernacular as they be. Our vernaculars do challenge one another, clash and scrape against one another. The principal language of Quebec is French, not English, because language carries in its train an entire culture and way of life. We must find a way to live so that when a person from one religious tradition rubs up against another's vernacular worldview, both believers might be enriched and enabled to live in the same world at peace. We need to be able to recognize and appreciate the fact that the subjective and particular elements of an alien tradition may offer us otherwise unnoticed insights into our own religion as well as into the faith of the other.

This is not to stress vernacular expressions of faith to the exclusion of the silence that employs no language whatsoever. The cultural traditions of a faith are not themselves to be deified—that would negate their vernacular force and lead to a narrow clinging to form over life. Deep, unmediated, and inexpressible experiences do occur.[12] All the traditions agree that in moments of grace, moments perhaps almost unnoticed, a person may move apart from all mediated meanings. No language. No culture. No words. No images. For those moments, one abides in simple and pure consciousness, sharply aware of the mystery surrounding us all. Still, when after such a wordless experience we turn back to worlds mediated by meaning, we do make the attempt to describe the mystery in terms familiar to us from our own vernacular culture.

However profound the experience, it remains beyond all words to describe and is not available as data. It demonstrates neither that all experiences are the same, nor that they are different. Neither does it signify

---

12. Keenan, *Meaning of Christ*, 188–96. Lonergan, *Method in Theology*, 106.

that all is a gray and tasteless neutrality. Mystics in each and every tradition witness to deep, life-wrenching experiences. And yet I am reluctant to identify those experiences as the foundation for a unity between all religions, or to claim that all religions are equal because all are grounded on such an experiential base, although I would strongly affirm the fundamental equality of all humans. But that is a conventional judgment and appeals to no unmediated insight or experience. Rather, it flows directly from our cultural, political, and legal demands as world citizens. Precisely because unmediated states of awareness are unmediated, such experiences—no matter how significant or life changing for the individual—are not and cannot be adequately expressed. And thus they provide no information whatsoever. One simply cannot reason from what cannot be expressed in verbal insight and judgment.

Furthermore, it is unwise to argue that unmediated experience is the only aspect of a religion that is true and valuable, for that would be to demote all apologetics to inane ramblings about superficial verbal affirmations on the mysterious beyond.[13] Rather, we would do well to attend to the doctrines and teachings of the various traditions—not as something superficial, but as expressions of the very heart of what is really valuable and truly real.

Some scholars of religion argue against the very possibility of pure and unmediated experience. Steven Katz argues, from a neo-Kantian stance, against unmediated mystical experience. He says that because every mystic is enmeshed "in the fetters of tradition, history, and time, he must express what is truly inexpressible in the inadequate symbols and syntax of his particular faith community."[14] The experience itself and the means by which it is later expressed, Katz (and others) would hold, are both formed by the ideas and concepts that the mystic brings to the moment. Thus, the Hindu experience of Brahman and the Christian experience of God are not the same because from the beginning they understand and describe divinity differently. And a scholar of religion can only study the mystic's report of an experience, for no one can actually get into or fully understand the experience of another individual. Liberal Catholic theologian Edward Schillebeeckx agrees with Katz that there are

13. See Muck, *Mysterious Beyond*, 24–25.

14. Katz, in the unpaginated first paragraph of "Editor's Introduction," *Mysticism and Religious Traditions*. See also his "'Conservative' Character of Mystical Experience," 3–60, in the same volume.

no unmediated experiences, for all individuals are inscribed within the languages and cultures of their birth and growth.[15]

Others defend the existence of unmediated mystic experience. Robert Forman cogently contends that mystic states include every state of consciousness in which a person has attained the cessation of thinking, a state that transcends any mediation. He calls these states "pure consciousness events" and argues that they are not culturally constructed.[16] I would agree heartily with Forman that such pure consciousness events do occur, but I think that they can play no role in any philosophy or theology of religious plurality. Being pure from thought, they are unavailable for thinkers, who are always shaped by their personal and communal histories.[17] We have available only subsequent descriptions, and those certainly are not the pure experience. So, if we are not to employ wordless mystic experience as a bridge or as the common ground between different religious traditions, and if we cannot get outside our own vernacular to talk about faith, how are we ever to understand one another?

First, we need a deep and humble re-appropriation of the vernacular expression of our faith tradition. The more deeply one realizes the historicity—the genealogy and the legacy—of one's own faith tradition, the more precious it becomes, and the more humble one's proclamation becomes. Preaching to the unconverted will not disappear, for we are all—each in our own tradition—enjoined to preach our good news, but we can be humble and gentle about it. And we can acknowledge that deep, life-transforming conversions are not the exclusive product of any one tradition.

No overarching worldview is remotely adequate to describe the rich and thick tapestry of the world's faith traditions. When one sits quietly and meditatively in Kyoto's Nishihonganji Temple, in the shadowy vastness of its Buddha-infused space with the image of Amida far in the distance across a plain of tatami-matted floor, one may be granted a taste and feel of the Dharma that is beyond any description. When—at the start of

15. Schillebeeckx, *Christ*, 31–36.

16. Forman, *Mysticism, Mind, Consciousness*, 131–67.

17. I agree with Louis Roy, who throughout his *Mystical Consciousness*, argues convincingly—against constructivists like Katz—that transcendent experiences are not trapped or fettered by their context; rather they call attention to their "objective" while never providing knowledge about that "object." See also Roy's *Transcendent Experiences*, 173.

the Easter-eve Vigil at Philadelphia's St. Norbert's Abbey—the fifteen-foot flame that is the newly-come light of Christ suddenly pierces the darkness of the high-arched nave, incarnational images may be inscribed onto one's brain and indeed into the very marrow of one's bones.[18]

Religions are rich and thick, available only in part to enunciation and analysis. Rather than seeking some bland, universal—even transcendent—common denominator among the many faiths, we need to cherish their differences. We must savor and preserve their distinctive textures, colors, flavors, aromas, images, and harmonies—and the inchoate insights that these engender in the depths of our quieted minds.

There is a pressing need for a philosophy of grounded faith that will affirm truth to be practiced while respecting and even revering the different truths affirmed and practiced by others. All our truths come textured, and all are to be acknowledged and valued. In order to succeed, a philosophy of religions must attune itself to particular faiths and specific traditions, each with its own historical, cultural, and linguistic peculiarities.

Developing new apologetics

There comes a time when it is necessary to re-articulate a faith—that is, to offer a new apologetic. This need arises again and again over time, in part because of the persistent tendency of cultures to domesticate religious practice, to mold it to a society's biases and preferences, and thereby to eviscerate its original sharp-edged challenge. The Christian believer comes to be seen as unthinkingly committed to "organized" religion, while the Buddhist practitioner may be regarded perhaps as vaguely wise but detached. Cultural filters functioning in place of intelligent inquiry provide simplistic images of stodgy Christians gathering in outmoded institutions, and otherworldly Buddhists meditating on riddles that have no answers. Reduced to stereotypes, neither of these faith tracks is seen to offer a rigorous path of practice that might engage life and death is-

---

18. Note the following observation by Bill Moyers: "I am grateful to have first been exposed to those qualities in my own Christian tradition. T. S. Eliot believed that 'no man [or woman] has ever climbed to the higher stages of the spiritual life who has not been a believer in a particular religion, or at least a particular philosophy.' As we dig deeper into our own religion, we are likely to break through to someone else digging deeper toward us from their own tradition, and on some metaphysical level, we converge, like the images inside a kaleidoscope, into new patterns of meaning that illuminate our own journey." Speech at Occidental College, February 7, 2007.

sues, enable one to touch God, or effect human transformation through a complete reorientation of consciousness.

When religious traditions lose their edge but still seem to claim exclusive truth for themselves to the denigration of others, it is no wonder that thoughtful people reject commitment to those faith communities. More and more they relegate spiritual questions to the personal realm and see faith as a matter of individual taste and choice. In the prevailing commonsense spirituality, no particular choice is to be privileged over another, and so all paths are regarded as equally relevant—and equally irrelevant. All as a result tend to lose their saving or awakening power.[19]

Unfortunately, this denuded understanding of faith and tradition as a matter of personal taste—albeit happily liberated from sectarian hatred and bias—leaves little space for passionate engagement and often falls victim to equally pernicious cultural and ethnic biases. Without engagement there remains little room for preaching the truth of any faith, or commending that truth to others as a valid path to follow. In the end, the entire world of religious tradition appears bland and tasteless. This, I would submit, is the challenge to writing any philosophy or theology of religions today. This challenge is new in that it demands that we eschew both culturally arrogant claims for an all-engulfing, single truth and the just as culturally arrogant claims of a vague and porous pluralism.

It is in part pressure from believers and practitioners feeling puzzled and challenged by the pluralist world that pushes theologians today to restate and reaffirm the faith of their particular tradition. But they must do so with a newly sharpened awareness of a world of many faiths, which raises important new questions about truth, culture, and language. These questions require religious thinkers to pull back from facile repetitions of long-affirmed truths and to look to the unplumbed depths of their faith.

Only by regarding our own traditions with new eyes can we as Christians, or as Buddhists, effectively preach the truth of that faith. Only thereby can we develop an appropriate apologetic that will address the barrier questions that discourage entry into any faith practice in this pluralist age. But, when we turn to delve deeper into our doctrinal histories, we often run right up against our own ignorance. We notice some fuzzy oversights that in the past have led us to affirm without understanding, confess without thinking, and preach without meaning.

19. See Keenan, "New Interfaith Context," 27–36.

Sometimes, and to our own surprise, we discover that even the languages and images of our own tradition are foreign to us. Cultures change, assumptions alter, vernaculars evolve, and new languages are added. Very few Christians today are conversant with the Greek language and thought patterns of the early Church. Few Jews go beyond the Hebrew they learn for their Bar Mitzvah or Bat Mitzvah, and few Buddhists can read either the Sanskrit or classical Chinese texts that explicate Nāgārjuna's philosophy of emptiness and dependent arising.

Over time, major alterations take place in the cultural surroundings of a religious tradition, while its orthodox language and doctrine tend to remain static. But although the accepted meanings of a religion are slow to change, they can indeed be affected by the cultural and linguistic shifts and historical evolutions taking place around it. Even doctrines and orthodoxies can and do change and evolve. Bernard Lonergan describes this process: "Slowly and gradually they are clarified, expressed, formulated, defined, only to be enriched and deepened and transformed, and no less often to be impoverished, emptied out, and deformed."[20]

So it is that eventually the thinkers of a religious tradition will find themselves faced with the task of re-articulating the tenets of their faith for a new age. They are called to state the doctrines of their faith tradition in a manner meaningful to, and addressing the concerns of, a culture that has evolved over time, adopting new patterns of attentiveness and a new awareness of where to find meaning.[21] At best, this re-articulation of faith will result not in some uninformed watering down of doctrine to appeal to contemporary tastes. It should instead express a constant deepening of faith and doctrine through the lived practice of the incarnate Church, in the awakened depths of everyday Zen living. Without negating or discarding ancient creeds and doctrines, the theologian must attempt always to plumb the depths of those creeds and doctrines and to re-present their truth within ever-shifting world realms.

In the case of Christianity, so long as the central affirmations about Christ and God are perceived to denigrate non-Christians, these will

20. Lonergan, *Method in Theology*, 79. See Crowe, *Lonergan Enterprise*, "Introduction." Lonergan calls for a personal appropriation of our own conscious activity so that we might perform such tasks with intention and skill.

21. Loy, *Awareness Bound and Unbound*, 2, on the usage of the terms "awareness" and "attention" as preferable renderings for the more common "mind" and "consciousness" in Buddhist texts.

be stumbling blocks to the common sense of the world in this current age. All too often, the doctrine of the Incarnation is misunderstood as primarily a claim that Jesus "our founder" is clearly the best among the founders of religions, because he is divine. This central Christian doctrine of Incarnation—that Christ while fully human was of one substance with God the Father—is very difficult even for many Christians today to understand or accept without hesitation. It is based on the Greek philosophical axiom, shared by the early Fathers of the Christian Church, that all individuals participate in their ideal form, which alone is true and real.[22] In that Greek context, whatever is said of Christ is also affirmed of Christians.[23] What Christ as the paradigm of essential humanness is by nature we are—or can become—by grace, that is, deified. So the incarnation of the Word means that the very nature of human nature is transfigured and assumed by grace into the life of God—the human nature of everyone, everywhere.

The early understanding of Incarnation was not based on images of Jesus as near and available. He is not a mythical hero figure or our secret pal, and yet many people imagine Jesus as such and thank him both for salvation in church on Sunday morning and for a touchdown in the stadium on Sunday afternoon. The faith of America, according to the provocative Alan Bloom, is a kind of "Jesusism."[24] This is the kind of faith that Janice Joplin sings of when she promises Jesus to make amends and begs him to give her that Mercedes Benz, because all her friends drive Porsches.

Since we no longer think in the same way that the ancient Greeks did, we have to struggle long and hard to comprehend the Incarnation as they did.[25] An understanding of all of this must be earned by dint of diligent study and extensive reading. We did not learn it in catechism or in Sunday school, and it is not necessarily available to us now on Sunday morning in church. A re-articulation of the doctrine of the Incarnation is one of the many challenges facing a theologian who would write a Christian apologetic for the present age.

22. Dodd, *Interpretation of the Fourth Gospel*, 139–40 and 170–79.

23. Meyendorff, *Christ in Eastern Christian Thought*, 15–18. See also his article, "The Nicene Creed," 1–19.

24. Bloom, *Jesus and Yahweh*, 89–95 and 127–64.

25. Haight, *Jesus*, 202–14 and 301–490, strives to reiterate this same sense by his newly structured Christology as the mediational symbol for this day.

Similar issues confront Buddhist thinkers. For example, there is the question of whether the awakening of the paradigmatic Buddha really is possible for us humans through practice of the path. Who cares if he was awakened so many centuries ago if we cannot likewise be awakened here and now? The very possibility of an awakening that leads to bliss for no-self and compassion for others seems alien and chimerical to many contemporary Buddhist practitioners, for they have not had the time or opportunity either to engage in serious meditation or to study the long and culturally complex history of Mahāyāna Buddhism.

Many lay practitioners pray to Buddhas and Bodhisattva savior figures as the presence of Other Power in their lives, without ever giving a thought to the emptiness of all buddhas and bodhisattvas. With a doctrinally shallow understanding, modern Buddhist practitioners try to gain merit and lessen the force of bad karma on their present and future lives. Few attend to Nāgārjuna's philosophy of emptiness, which would empty the idea of merit altogether and equate the buddhas with the everyday mind of ordinary people. Like the Christians, those who would articulate a Buddhist apologetics for the modern age also have their challenges.

Moreover, no apologetic today can be written in isolation from or in ignorance of traditions other than the theologian's own. In-depth study and understanding of other religious traditions are prerequisites for writing any effective apologetic to address this pluralist world. This involves diligent and sophisticated historical and intellectual work but, unfortunately, most theologians and clergy in the various faith traditions are either disinclined or ill equipped to take up this challenge. Within their own inner circles of doctrinal learning, they rarely feel impelled to entertain seriously the doctrines of other faiths.

For one thing, the doctrines of other religions often bring into question one's own accepted norms of universally valid truth. I well remember being surprised when my professor of scholastic philosophy admitted that actually he had never read anything of Kant, for he was convinced a priori that Kant's idealism was wrong. Not very responsibly, I suppose, I inherited his attitude and have tended to regard Kantians as not worthy of much study or effort. Biases give birth to biases. Moreover, in order to understand the doctrines of other religions, one has to take up the vital study of entire new languages and cultures of meaning and that is hard work. It is not a task that appeals to already defined and accomplished theologians. Very often, theologians and clergy alike simply choose to withdraw into their accustomed faith culture and its community, vaguely open-minded perhaps, but not reaching out to engage with "others."

The result is unfortunate not only in terms of interfaith understanding, but also in terms of people giving serious consideration to the faith that is commended by these communities and their leaders. Our modern global culture will filter out from even brief consideration any belief that fails to address the test of tolerance and mutual respect. By not engaging the question of religious pluralism, by ignoring its vital importance, religious thinkers and leaders render moot any restated apologetics they may offer for their faith. In the face of their silence on that issue, many people will simply forego entry into a tradition they perceive as usurping truth for itself alone.

In order to articulate any new religious apologetic—whether in defense of a particular tradition or of religious traditions in general—we need a philosophy of how we human beings arrive at truth. What is the relationship between faith and truth? Between scripture and reason? If such issues are not addressed, they will become gateway closures, obstacles that hinder people from embarking upon paths of practice that can lead them toward true and authentic living. We need to discuss these "gateway" questions openly. What is required is a philosophy of religious truth that is accessible and acceptable to all, without committing everyone to one faith or another.

Western theology has been described as faith seeking understanding (*fides quaerens intellectum*). This is usually seen as a movement from truth, already received in scripture and confessed in traditional faith, to an understanding of the meaning and ramifications of that affirmation. Similarly, Chinese Buddhist texts translate the Sanskrit term for "faith commitment" (*adhimukti*) as "faith + understanding" (*hsin-chieh*; 信 解), suggesting that they see commitment as a movement that begins first with faith and then passes into understanding—and finally to awakening.

This pattern reflects, I think, our actual experience: Faith is pure gift, which begins with enticements toward transcendence and hints at a wisdom deeper than words, and so the movement from faith toward understanding starts from within a given tradition. Such a faith movement toward transcendence remains unsignified, and therefore free from the postmodern critique that decries any transcendental signified or unquestionable realm as the core validator for our ideas and words. Signified transcendence is domesticated and misused transcendence. Even the medievals knew that we point toward God, but do not know what God is or means. Faith comes first, and all subsequent attempts to understand that which lies beyond are inevitably grounded (consciously or not) upon culturally embedded preconceptions of just how the universe fits together and who we all are. The cultural and metaphysical assumptions underlying a tradition shape our perceptions in such a way that it is quite difficult to get outside that framework to consider a tradition's validity in the modern—or indeed the postmodern—sense of a cultural critique. But this is precisely what is needed.

For our apologetic task, we need a critical philosophy of religious consciousness that will embrace both deep readings of many different faith traditions as well as dialogue between people of different faiths.[26] And this philosophy of religions must be able to recommend itself to people who do not share its culture or any of its embedded faiths.

From there, we in each tradition must move to offer a reasonable account of the particular faith that is in us, developing an apologetic to defend the truth of that faith within its culturally-given context and to recommend that others respect and honor that faith, even perhaps that they accept it for themselves, so long as that is freely their decision. I have never been insulted by, nor taken umbrage at, an intelligent Buddhist missionary. Rather, I have felt honored that he or she would take the time to enunciate to me what he or she holds most dear and precious. For, surely, people within each tradition—grounded in its vernacular culture and offering an apologetic expressed in its own languages—are warranted by tradition and clear thinking to confess and experience their faith and to practice it as a valid and sure guide for living and dying. They should be able robustly and unapologetically to believe and to preach that their own faith tradition in all its particularity is indeed ultimate, for ultimate reality is not just some vague overarching philosophical truth that can be uncovered by privileged interfaith theologians. We are all called to preach the gospel, teach the Dharma of the Buddha, and announce to the world the oneness of Allah.

I have found in the philosophies of Mahāyāna Buddhism a perspective that I believe can be adopted in this endeavor. In the following chapter, I shall introduce the facets of these philosophies that may be of most use in crafting a new philosophy of religions.

26. Such is the plea of Fredericks, *Faith among Faiths*, 169–79, for a creative tension beyond tolerance that engenders friendships and feeds on hope for the future.

45

3

The Useful Philosophies of Mahāyāna Buddhism

The distinction between Buddhist doctrine
and Mahāyāna philosophy

ACH AND EVERY PHILOSOPHY, like each and every faith, grows from
within its surrounding culture. And no philosophy of religion, whether rigorously rational or faith inspired, developed entirely apart from a
particular religious tradition. A philosophy of religions, when it looks at
the many other religions in the world, necessarily employs categories that
are familiar to its own tradition. No philosophical category is meta-his-
torical, or meta-religious.

A philosophy of religion must therefore function in full awareness
of its cultural origins. It will not do for Christians to assert that the
Fatherhood of God entails the revelation of God to other, non-Christian
traditions, such that those traditions are thereby also efficacious. Some
of those other traditions do not embrace a doctrine of God at all, either
as Father or as revealer. Buddhism, for example, offers no intelligent discourse on God and never speaks about divine Fatherhood. Similarly, it
will not do for Buddhists to assume that all Christian references to God
as ultimate are equivalent to deluded (in the Buddhist view) Hindu ideas
about the Almighty Creator Īśvāra. The Hindu creator god—tradition-
ally critiqued by Buddhists as one being within the order of beings—is
entirely different from theistic affirmations of God as ultimate.[1]

1. Schmidt-Leukel, *Christianity, Buddhism, and the Question of Creation*, 143–78. See
Lonergan, *Method in Theology*, 214–220, on cultural differences, which he distinguished
into three: (1) perspectival and cultural, wherein statements that verbally contradict one
another may not be truly exclusionary, but merely perspectival; (2) genetic differences,
in which things differ along a common line of growth, and (3) dialectical, or truly exclusionary differences. In such a context the difference between Īśvara and God is indeed

However, the philosophy underpinning Mahāyāna Buddhism differs from most other philosophical approaches to religious thinking in one important way: It focuses not upon the *content* that is understood but rather upon the *act* of understanding. Thus, even though Mahāyāna philosophy is grounded historically in Indian Buddhism, its insights into religious understanding can be recommended for broader application, beyond and apart from the theological doctrines of any tradition, even its own.[2] An appreciation for the Mahāyāna themes of emptiness and dependent arising, the two truths of worldly convention and ultimate meaning, and its critical understanding of mind does not require one to take refuge in the Buddha, accepting his description of the world in the Four Noble Truths[3] or committing to the Eightfold Path of Buddhist practice. This Mahāyāna philosophy directs attention to understanding all faith acts and practices. It offers an interpretation of the *way* in which we humans come to religious understanding and so is not at all limited to Buddhism.

Two branches of Mahāyāna philosophy in particular—the Middle Path (or Mādhyamika) and the Yogācāra—offer artful explanations of the mind of truth and understanding, and these explanations are potentially quite useful in the construction of a philosophy of religions. A philosophy of religion employing Mahāyāna understandings would hold that no single viewpoint can ever encompass accurately the world's plurality of religions, for no viewpoint has a vantage point (an advantage) from which it can experience all the traditions or gain true insight into the doctrine and practice of other peoples' faiths. No single perspective is ever capable

---

perspectival, for no one who has studied the tract *De Deo Uno* (On the One God) could possibly recognize the God therein described as anything like the Hindu or Buddhist notions of gods, who are within the cycle of transmigration and rather like powerful angels in Jewish and Christian mythology.

2. Compare Lonergan, *Insight*, where he too explicates a critical philosophy of consciousness, which gladdened my spirit in school days. I was disappointed later, though, that his privately published books on theology reversed the movement that he had described from experience to insight to judgment, claiming that the truth of faith has already been revealed, so that we need only to gain insight into it and experience it in our lives. The human élan to reach out infinitely has here been stifled by lopping off the faith inspired judgments about revealed truth. Some of his students from Rome's Gregorian University used to apologize for him, reporting that he himself said teaching there hamstrung him.

3. These are the truths that (1) all is suffering; (2) suffering arises from causes: an ongoing cycle beginning with primal ignorance; (3) there is a cessation of that suffering, which is (4) the path whereby one can attain that cessation.

of rendering judgment about other religions. A Mahāyāna philosophy of religions is a no-philosophy. It is a philosophy that empties philosophy.[4]

Mahāyāna philosophy addresses itself to all who have minds and seek to understand. This philosophy does of course underlie and support many different expressions of the Buddhist religious tradition that find faith embodiment variously in the Buddha Amitābha, the Buddha Mahāvairocana, the Bodhisattva Bodhidharma, and in all the richly textured symbols and practices of the Pure Land, Shingon, and Zen schools of Buddhism. But the philosophy of Mahāyāna is singularly capable of stepping outside its historical Buddhist context and offering support to any faith tradition that would attempt to explicate faith in understanding.

It is true that the main categories of this philosophy do originate in a central practice of Mahāyāna Buddhism—that of emptiness and truth. Yet this practice focuses inward to critique and analyze the human mind that understands and practices a faith tradition, rather than looking outward to emphasize the object of that mind's understanding. It draws attention to the radical transience of all things—none of which can sustain themselves as self-enclosed and self-supporting entities and none of which can resist the passing flow of time and the permutations of culture. It acknowledges that even religious doctrine develops out of a variety of cultural causes and conditions.

Mahāyāna offers a theory of being—an ontology—that is always on the point of disappearing. It is much more concerned with meditative practice than with statements about the origin and structure of the universe (metaphysics). In its perspective, it is enough if a tradition leads us into the deep awakening of ultimate silence and divine wonder, and then brings us back again to engage in tasks of intelligence and compassion in this world. In Christian terms, it is enough if faith in Christ identifies us with the incarnate Word, leads us into the divine presence, and thereby moves us to announce that the kingdom of justice and peace is already near, already here, and to work for that realization. This is true religion, not a mere cultural construct. It is absolutely and fully true. In different

4. The scholarly culture of India is much more systematic and analytically than the subsequent Buddhist enculturation in China, with its already influential Taoist and Confucian heritage. China embraces a philosophy of organism and its philosophers seem always to write forcefully and poetically, not so much analytically. See Lai, "Mahāyāna Reading of Chalcedon Christology," 209–30, for an alternate Mahāyāna approach to reading Christology in terms of Tathāgatagarbha and Buddha Nature traditions, which I would indeed support enthusiastically.

theological terms, it may lead us to touch God, or to become awakened as a buddha. And just as true religion is more a preparation for awakening than a map of metaphysical reality, so Mahāyāna philosophy refuses to objectify even itself as some set of privileged doctrines about the real.

It is for these reasons that I would suggest this philosophy as an appropriate resource for developing a philosophy of religions in a pluralist world.

The development of Mahāyāna philosophy

Mahāyāna philosophy was developed over several centuries in India and East Asia by a number of thinkers and practitioners of the Middle Path (Mādhyamika) and Yogācāra schools—by Nāgārjuna, Āryadeva, and Candrakīrti, by Asaṅga, Vasubandhu, and Dharmapāla.[5] The Middle Path branch of this philosophy focuses upon emptiness and its shocking negations, while the Yogācāra branch gives particular attention to the structure and functioning of the human mind that understands emptiness.

Mahāyāna, the Great (*mahā*) Vehicle (*yāna*) of Buddhism, arose in opposition to an earlier Indian Buddhist philosophy called Abhidharma. Abhidharma's philosophical theory mapped out a clear, metaphysical path toward the blissful cessation of all suffering, or *nirvāna*. But Mahāyāna thinkers rejected this Abhidharma diagram of the path of Buddhist practice, denigrating it as "Hīnayāna," a lesser (*hīna*) vehicle (*yāna*). The Mahāyānists argued that these earlier Buddhist teachers, in insisting on the correctness of their path, had lost the way to awakening. They criti-

5. Mahāyāna philosophy developed beyond the schools herein described into the Indian and Tibetan Logic Tradition (Pramāṇavāda), but this tradition was not much transmitted into China or Japan, and what remains of them in East Asian languages presents a vocabulary almost impossible to decipher. Scholars of Mahāyāna Buddhism take two established tracks in their endeavors. Those who focus on Indian and Tibetan languages and cultures track the development of Buddhist philosophy from Mādhyamika and Yogācāra to the Pramāṇavāda, the logic and epistemology of Dharmakīrti, the great seventh century Indian philosopher. Those who concentrate on East Asian languages and cultures trace Indian Buddhist thought through Mādhyamika and Yogācāra and then, bypassing the Buddhist logical traditions as too fuzzy, move into the Chinese, Korean, and Japanese traditions. Such an attitude in part is culturally conditioned by the study of Chinese thought and culture, and in part the bias of those who do not understand and cannot follow the torturous arguments of the Pramāṇa traditions and their modern interpreters. For the clearest explanation of these traditions, see Dreyfus, *Recognizing Reality*, and Dunne, *Foundations of Dharmakīrti's Philosophy*.

cized them for affirming with their mouths what they failed to realize in the depth of their hearts and minds.

The very earliest layer of Buddhist teachings championed "no-self," the absence of any internal core being that a person might lay claim to as one's very own. But the Mahāyānists pointed out that even people who profess this doctrine of no-self still manage to cling to the self through attachment to other things. One of those attachments could even be to Buddhist doctrine, if they hold insistently to the absolute correctness of its self-defining and self-supporting truth. To counter this tendency—and urge us not to cling to self in the guise of commitments to other things—the Mahāyāna path makes its goal the attainment of a wisdom that realizes no-self in *every* aspect of life. This wisdom comes in two kinds: The first is the quiet root wisdom of otherworldly non-discrimination. The second kind of wisdom is "subsequently attained" and is expressed through one's reengagement in the world.

From the earliest days of Buddhist teaching, practitioners sought a quiet and otherworldly understanding of no-self, in emulation of the Buddha Śākyamuni's awakening. This awakened wisdom was a realization that our sense of self (and, by extension, our sense of our traditions and religions) is based upon nothing solid, but instead is a construct composed of a great variety of contributing factors. The sense of who we are is built up in part from all the benevolent factors of our common and personal past and at the same time is debased by the effects of greed, anger, and delusion—the three poisons. These negative effects might be virulent and active in our present lives, or they might be latent—the lingering results of long ago actions (*karma*).

The wisdom of no-self reverberates through all the patterns of Mahāyāna Buddhist thinking, invariably turning the focus inward, toward the mind that can be awakened, for mind is the most human aspect of all that makes us human. This early Buddhist doctrine of no-self was developed to some extent as a response to prior Hindu assertions that our true being is not who we are as individuals but is rather the great Self (*ātman*), which in fact is one and the same as the ultimately real reality (*brahman*). But the Buddha swept away that whole Hindu description of reality. He declared instead that our being is constituted by the maturation of many previous actions, stretching back far beyond anyone's ability to reckon, and that this being or self lacks any abiding core of reality.

Still, everywhere and always—regardless of culture—people seem to have a penchant for assuming the precious importance of their inner self. In our culture, it is not uncommon to hear people speak of "Number One"—I, myself, the center of my universe. We hear talk of self-actualization, honoring our inner child, maximizing our individual potential. The Buddha, by stark contrast, insisted that this everyday self with whom we are so preoccupied is entirely empty of any abiding reality—there *is* no inner self to nurture or to protect or to maximize. (Were this view to be widely accepted by American culture today, entire sections of our bookstores and libraries would become irrelevant!)

The "Perfection of Wisdom" movement in Mahāyāna Buddhism took this teaching of no-self even farther. Its scriptures[6] proclaim that the concept of no-self undercuts not just our assumption that there exists a substantive everyday self, but it undercuts as well any and all philosophic views, for even if we affirm no-self we can still project our selfhood upon tribe, religion, nation, or even just upon being right. "Perfected" wisdom would negate all metaphysics, all views, and all philosophies that presume to describe reality. It makes a view-canceling recommendation for non-discriminative wisdom, the wisdom that recognizes the emptiness of all things—all views, all human constructs, indeed the entire world in all its forms and all its aspects.

The Perfection of Wisdom texts teach that the first thing we mistake for selfhood is physical form. But physical form—like every other purported constituent of selfhood—is in fact empty. Empty, too, are the goal of cessation and the suffering of transmigration—indeed all Buddhist doctrines. There is nothing to be identified as core Buddhist doctrine, for there is no core to anything, anywhere.

And yet, proclaims the *Heart Scripture* in apparent self-contradiction, this very emptiness *is* form. The absence of any core doctrine is precisely the import of Mahāyāna doctrine. Truth is not attained by choosing one opinion over another but rather through the rejection of all opinion. Only after doctrine and opinion are utterly rejected may they then be reclaimed as guides on the path to a nowhere that is richer than any somewhere might ever be. In this way, wisdom is first of all fundamental, otherworldly non-discrimination. But this otherworldly wisdom must be followed by the subsequent attainment of a wisdom that is able

---

6. The *Eight Thousand Verses, Diamond Cutter,* and *Heart Scriptures.*

to function in the world—a conventional wisdom. An awakened one, a buddha, thus abides both in the quietude that is beyond all ideas and judgments and in the teaching of doctrine to, and compassionate aid of, beings in this world.

Of the two branches of Mahāyāna thinking that we propose to employ in developing a new philosophy of religions, the Middle Path—or Mādhyamika—emphasizes two inter-related themes. Its first theme is the equation of emptiness with "dependent arising" (the coming-to-be of all things out of a myriad of contributing causes and conditions). The second important theme of the Middle Path is the disjunction between two kinds of truth—the truth of ultimate meaning and the truth of worldly convention.

A later branch of Mahāyāna called Yogācāra (referring to the practice of yogic meditation) expands on these same themes and adds a critical analysis of human consciousness. The Yogācārins, in seeking to understand the origins of delusion as well as the means of conversion to awakening and wisdom, detail the structure of both conscious and unconscious levels of mind. They also outline three patterns in which the human mind functions.[7]

THE MIDDLE PATH OF MĀDHYAMIKA

The philosophy of emptiness

In Buddhist doctrine, our attachment to a false self is the obstacle that blocks faith and awakening. But it is not enough merely to negate the self in words. Our very sense of being here in this world is intimately intertwined with the notion of having an inner core around which we move with surety and comfort. Indeed, we are entirely capable of verbally affirming the doctrine of no-self even as we continue to live a self-centered life. One begins to comprehend how very difficult it is to negate the self when the Buddhist teachers insist that more is required of us: Beyond negating the individual self, we must also negate any sense of "me and mine." If we fail to root out this attitude, we are likely to project

---

7. Among the proliferating studies on these philosophies, my scholarly mentors have been Richard Robinson, Frederick Streng, C.W. Huntington, Gadjin Nagao, Kyōo Nishio, Susumu Yamaguchi, Jikidō Takasaki, Minoru Kiyota, Mervyn Sprung—some of whose works are mentioned in the bibliography.

a mutated and camouflaged notion of self onto our family, or group, or nation, or even onto our religion, in a kind of shared delusion and common madness.

This kind of madness is often evident in times of military conflict. It is not by mere coincidence that the conduct of war is carried out in accordance with military "doctrine," for what is at stake is the very meaning of our lives, everything that we hold dear. Armies commonly depend upon providing a viable sense of self to young people who are just coming of age, offering them a cause with which to identify. Not all martyrs are self-less heroes—often they are simply persons desperately and sadly dying in search of some deluded dream of a greater self.

Often—indeed usually—individuals cherish and defend their self-identity. But the undeniable fact is that any self—even group-identified or faith-inspired—is a construct of its time and place. Sometimes we try to obscure this fact with illusions of glory and sacrifice. Indeed, our languages and cultures offer us a myriad of ways to build protective barriers against the fear that our inner selves might actually be empty of any abiding permanence. They shield us from the suspicion that we are ever on the brink of fading into long-forgotten history, of falling into an abyss of nothingness.

The Mahāyāna project calls attention to all manner of human subterfuges for self-clinging. We may, for example, negate the self but still cling to a self-supporting and self-validating religious orthodoxy—to our Buddhist, or Christian, or Jewish identity. This is why the leading Middle Path philosopher Nāgārjuna denied the validity of *all* views, even the views most central to Buddhist doctrine, for no view can serve as the locator of anyone's being.[8] Nāgārjuna would thus go so far as to deny the validity of basic Buddhist doctrines like the difference between transmigration through endless sufferings (*saṃsāra*) and the blissful cessation of all that ongoing pain (*nirvāna*); the difference between the awakened Buddha and deluded persons; the five constituents falsely regarded as the self; and even the Four Noble Truths first articulated by the historical Buddha—suffering, the origin of suffering, the cessation of suffering, and the path whereby that is realized.

---

8. See Garfield, *Fundamental Wisdom*, 293–321 and his *Empty Words*, 46–68, on emptiness and views. Also Nagao, *Foundational Standpoint*, 85–96 and his "What Remains in Śūnyatā," in Kiyota, *Mahāyāna Buddhist Meditation*, 66–82.

Viewpoints (including religious doctrines) are of necessity expressed in language, and Mahāyāna teaches that human language is itself evanescent and unfixed, its meanings changing over time. Basic college dictionaries give us the etymology of a word and define its meaning in clear and concise terms. But take a look at the *Unabridged Oxford English Dictionary*. It cites all ascertainable usages of an English word from the earliest discoverable example on down through time and over space. Reading the entries in this massive dictionary, it is easy to see how the meanings of words shift and flow in ever-changing contexts. Although some meanings and usages of a word may have evolved in traceable patterns, the origins of other expressions are lost in the mists of passing time and changing contexts. When philologists attempt to reconstruct the career of a word over time, they become archaeologists excavating the many historical levels of human consciousness.

Like a word, a particular viewpoint can be useful and valid within its context of supporting experiences and insights. But, taken apart from its culture, context, and language of origin, any viewpoint loses clear and certain validity. It can claim to be a true judgment only in virtue of a multitude of prior insights and experiences that are tied to a particular cultural milieu. To cling to a viewpoint—even the most orthodox of viewpoints or the most patriotic of sentiments—as if somehow it captures the very essence of things and expresses a perennial and universal truth is to occlude awakening. Such self-assured declaration of the truth exalts our human sense of who we are as proud carriers of an absolute faith tradition or a patriotic dream (for God and country). Clinging to any such viewpoint, the Mahāyānists tell us, is but another way to cling to the self and to preclude insight.

Like the early Christian tradition of apophatic theology—the mystical theology that speaks (*phases*) only by negating and taking away (*apo*) concepts and images—Middle Path philosophy advises us first to draw back from the world of language and culture. Then, when we return to engage once more in the realm where meanings are expressed in words, we are better prepared to relate to that world and its many issues and problems, albeit with a chastened sense of the limits of our human language and understanding. No avenue is to be left open for intellectual pretense or pride. There are to be no Mahāyāna parades or rallies, no Mahāyāna political parties or lobby groups.

This philosophy is not some kind of anti-intellectual program, but it does demand that we start by acknowledging that any absolute truth claim is a dead-end impasse. It presses upon us the raw recognition that every experience, idea, and viewpoint functions only in terms of its own context and only as a more-or-less adequate statement of truth. Only after we reach that realization can our thinking and speaking reclaim their true validity in humbled humanness. Only then can our words embody and express true and valid doctrine.

At that point, we are ready to reenter the world where meaning is mediated through a particular language and culture. In that world, we may then carry out the tasks of a bodhisattva—a "wisdom-being" moved by compassion to aid and teach other beings, to heal the suffering and the pain without proffering yet another "true" viewpoint or some new program of action. The basis or foundation of this Middle Path is that there *is* no foundation. No intellectual map will suffice to delineate the path. No picture can represent what is really real. All views are empty, for no view corresponds to anything that is solid and enduring.

The Middle Path in its description of all viewpoints and all things as empty recalls the Spanish mystic John of the Cross and his ever-urgent identification of all things as "nothing." They are but obstacles on the ascent to the spiritual mountain of union with God. Every attachment must fall away, says John, for no matter how thin the cord that binds, still it prevents the soul from taking flight from the things of this world. The *Perfection of Wisdom* scriptures, which marked the rise of Mahāyāna and set the framework for all Mahāyāna thinkers, breathe the same air as Jewish and Christian mystics. But whereas Jewish and Christian mystic traditions have occupied only a very marginal place in the development of Western religious thought, the mystic thrust of Mahāyāna Buddhism was central to all its later endeavors. It supported the intricate but compelling Middle Path dialectic and effectively resisted the tendency of intellectual mapping to usurp spiritual practice.

And so Middle Path philosophy maintains that all viewpoints are empty of any essential definition, for things themselves possess no essence. As all we human beings learn sooner or later, in one way or another, this world is a constant and unending flow of radical impermanence and change, offering no firm foothold. No anchor to tie us down. No seabed to accept any anchor. No self that needs to be anchored.

Emptiness as dependent arising

According to Mahāyāna philosophy, each one of us begins in primal ignorance, confined to a knowledge of our own experience, which generally entails suffering of one kind or another. That suffering, the Buddha taught, results from actions taken in the past—either our own actions or those taken by others before us. We might, for instance, have chosen to act in a way that promotes our own self-interest but at the same time harms another; sooner or later we may well suffer the consequences of that choice. Or perhaps our forebears acted to oppress another group of people; generations later, we may be the ones who pay the price for those injustices committed in the past. This is what the Buddhists call *karma*, which simply means "action."

So all our own past actions, as well as those of others, comprise the chain of karmic causation. And the convergence of these many different causes and conditions results in our experience of suffering in this life. Moreover, traditional Buddhist thought maintains, this applies not only to this lifetime; karma entangles us deluded beings in an endless cycle of rebirth and consequent further suffering over many lifetimes. And so the goal of early Buddhist practice (and this continued to be the focus in Theravada Buddhism[9]) was the cessation of the cycle of rebirth, liberation from suffering, and final peace for the practitioner.

To explain the chain of karmic causation and demonstrate how past actions converge to cause suffering in the present, Buddhist thinkers developed the doctrine of "dependent arising"—the understanding that any condition in this world *arises* from a multitude of factors that come into being in *dependence* upon one another. One can visualize this perhaps as several sticks standing together to form a kind of teepee, maintaining that position only because they are holding one another in place. Remove one, and the whole structure is likely to collapse. In this day of ecological consciousness, when we have become familiar with such expressions as "the web of life," this kind of interdependence is perhaps not too difficult for us to understand.

Over time, as people reflected on the Mahāyāna path, they began to see a deeper significance in dependent arising. Not only do all our delu-

9. The other main branch of Buddhism, prevalent in Sri Lanka and the countries of Southeast Asia. Mahāyāna ("Great Vehicle") Buddhists contrasted their goal of the salvation of *all* sentient beings to Theravada's emphasis on the liberation of the individual practitioner, and so characterized the latter as a "lesser vehicle," or "Hīnayāna."

sions and sufferings arise out of clusters of causes coming together over the long course of history, but indeed *all* things natural and human—even good things—arise in dependence upon a convergence of causes. Nothing abides fixedly and permanently. Sooner or later we are all endangered species. Empty of any fixed and self-enclosed essence, every thing and every person arises, and in time passes away, as the result of a host of causes and conditions.

Eventually, the Middle Path philosopher Nāgārjuna came to identify dependent arising with emptiness. He concluded that insight into the fact that all things arise in dependence upon one another follows directly from insight into the emptiness of all things. Everything arises as the result of a concatenation of causes and conditions = Nothing has an abiding core or essence.

For Nāgārjuna, to practice the Middle Path meant to attain precisely this insight.[10] But, he maintained, even that Middle Path of meditative insight is itself empty. In Mahāyāna thinking, not only the deluded entities of our experience are emptied of essence; so, too, are the very methods and aims of Mahāyāna practice. Cessation (*nirvāna*) is not a place "out there" or "up there," not a destination on a journey. Cessation, according to Nāgārjuna, is insight into emptiness, abiding neither there or here. And the path to that realization is dependently arisen. The essence-free being of that which exists does arise from multiple causes and conditions and does exist in our human world, and in that world we do engage in practices of wisdom that might lead to cessation that abides neither "up there" nor "down here."

Very much as we have recently become aware of the complex ecosystems that interact to support life on this planet, the Mahāyāna Buddhists came to see emptiness as signifying a deep, second dimension of the earlier doctrine of dependent arising. It is not just the dependent arising of suffering and pain. It is the dependent arising of all that is, of the passing beauty and the painful history of all of our lives.

The Middle Path, then, is the practice of holding the two—negative emptiness and positive dependent arising—in healthy and dynamic tension. We are to be engaged in this world without becoming caught in reifying views. To be in the world but not of the world. It is as though we are to balance on a tightrope without falling either into the negativity of

10. See Nagao, *Foundational Standpoint*, 85–107.

emptiness on the one side or, on the other, into the temptation to map reality along the lines of our own definitive views. Like an acrobat, we must try to maintain our balance, not statically, but by moving along the path limned by the rope.

There is great freedom in gaining insight into the empty, dependent arising of all things, for it removes the need to push oneself forward and carve out a niche for a self that really does not exist. The freedom of the saints of God is a freedom from self-centered living. This freedom demands engagement in the world in order to carry out the compassionate deeds of a "wisdom-being," a bodhisattva. The wisdom of emptiness flows into the engagement of compassion.[11]

The doctrine of emptiness is meant to enable us both to realize non-discriminative wisdom and also to influence our decisions and actions in the world—dissolving passions and desires that are based on our attachment to things as though they had their own self-existence. Its purpose is to assist the practitioner to gain insight into the fleeting nature of the self and to become aware that all things and all viewpoints are dependent upon transient causes and conditions.

Emptiness is not a word that indicates some substratum of ultimate reality. It is used by Nāgārjuna as a tool—a prod for breaking apart all claims to an identifiable metaphysical absolute.[12] It is meant, in other words, to shake our self-assurance that we possess a true and accurate map of reality. Nāgārjuna says that "it is a descriptive designation having recourse to dependent arising." As a "descriptive designation," emptiness is in effect an adjective,[13] and adjectives never have ontological status. Or perhaps it should be called an adverb, for emptiness describes *how* things exist—dependently and essence-free.[14]

As we have seen, Nāgārjuna introduced the term of emptiness by way of response to earlier Abhidharma philosophers' methods of regarding reality as the really real, out-there world that is perceived by our senses. To them, all that was necessary to describe reality was to correctly

---

11. Buddhists exercise that compassion today not only by teaching others how to escape this world of suffering, but also by undertaking tasks of social change and world-building. See Queen and King, *Engaged Buddhism*.

12. Streng, *Emptiness*, 155–80.

13. Huntington, *Emptiness of Emptiness*, 64–65.

14. Verse 22 of Nāgārjuna's *Vigrahavyavatāni*, in Streng, *Emptiness*, "Averting the Arguments," 224.

analyze the fundamental essences and definitions of things. If there is a similar element of this kind of objective realism in the way we understand the world today, then Nāgārjuna's critique may readily be applied in our modern context as well. Emptiness offers a means by which to critique the way we talk about reality.[15] It points out that the very manner in which we describe reality is basically flawed by our primal ignorance, which leads us humans to rely on rigid categories of religious narrow-minded delusion or national self-interest that are not nearly so stable as they look to us.

Emptiness itself is of course a conceptual term, belonging to a dependently arisen system of terms and ideas. A true picture of reality, the Middle Path philosopher will argue, is beyond any form of human conceptualization, any depiction of the real. It is a no-picture, a camera at rest. As Candrakīrti says, it is "the coming to rest of named things."[16] Words of necessity slice reality into pieces, offering us but fragmented impressions. The Middle Path's equation of emptiness and dependent arising works to refute all absolute viewpoints, without proposing any overarching, independent viewpoint that would encompass all. It forces us to abandon the thought that any philosophy is able to lay bare true reality for our inspection.

In short, emptiness does not refer to an objective reality. Candrakīrti, the chief commentator on Nāgārjuna's philosophy of no philosophy, clarifies this important point with a clever analogy:

> It is as if a shopkeeper said to a man: I have no goods at all to sell you. If this man were then to reply: Very well, then sell me your lack of goods for sale, how would this man be able to take hold of any goods?[17]

A negation of all viewpoints that claim to be absolute need not become a viewpoint in itself, just as it is impossible to purchase a "lack of goods for sale." On more than one occasion Nāgārjuna insists that:

> Emptiness is proclaimed by the victorious [Buddha] as the refutation of all viewpoints; but those who hold emptiness to be a viewpoint—the true sages have pronounced incurable.[18]

15. Candrakīrti, *Lucid Exposition*, 521.

16. Ibid., 248.

17. Ibid., 248.

18. Nāgārjuna, *Stanzas on the Middle*, 13:8.

In western terms, the Middle Path thinkers were much more concerned with *fides qua* than with *fides quae*—the mind with which one believes rather than the content believed. Nāgārjuna is not concerned with *what* we understand but with the existential impact of *how* we understand. He is not concerned with viewpoints themselves, but with how we arrive at and hold our viewpoints. If we approach with humility, we will not be caught in frozen views that mutate authentic practice.

Nāgārjuna denies that any definition or verbal representation can ever capture an objectively real part of reality. Words, he emphasizes, do not correspond to objective realities. Rather, they create boundaries that function for cultural purposes but when closely analyzed will simply fall apart. And viewpoints based on those words, when pushed far enough, will either implode from inconsistency or collapse from irrelevancy.

Although words do not correspond to objectively real categories, Nāgārjuna certainly does not deny that they can serve a purpose in this world. He himself uses many words! He does not discredit the use of words in making practical distinctions as we go about our daily lives, or even as we engage in the path toward awakening. Verbal distinctions are only false when they pretend to grasp the really real and to represent absolute truth. Dependent arising makes it clear that words and their definitions depend upon one another, so that any metaphysical system that makes use of words is also dependently arisen and therefore not absolute.

Metaphysical systems, which purport to describe the world as it really is, are themselves in fact dependent upon a multitude of factors. The answers they provide about the world depend on where they start. The way we see and understand things depends upon our cultural context, frame of reference, and even on the particular questions we ask. These things in turn differ from culture to culture.

Middle Path philosophy is quite as deconstructive as any French philosophy has ever been. Taking its lead from the *Perfection of Wisdom* scriptures, it reveals that metaphysical principles are, by nature, human constructs and thus can never be absolute. Metaphysical systems in their statements about reality always begin with their own basic assumptions and definitions, and from there construct an all-encompassing and absolute worldview. In describing the world, they fence their adherents within the interlocking meanings of the basic definitions with which they begin. But ultimate meaning can never exist inside such an enclosure: it is always entirely other, ineffable, and unattainable.

In the words of Jewish philosopher Abraham Joshua Heschel:

> The search of reason ends at the shore of the known; on the immense expanse beyond it only the sense of the ineffable can glide. It alone knows the route to that which is remote from experience and understanding. Neither of them is amphibious: reason cannot go beyond the shore, and the sense of the ineffable is out of place where we measure, where we weigh. We do not leave the shore of the known in search of adventure or suspense or because of the failure of reason to answer our questions. We sail because our mind is like a fantastic seashell, and when applying our ear to its lips we hear a perpetual murmur from the waves beyond the shore.
>
> Citizens of two realms, we all must sustain a dual allegiance: we sense the ineffable in one realm, we name and exploit reality in another. Between the two we set up a system of references, but we can never fill the gap. They are as far and as close to each other as time and calendar, as violin and melody, as life and what lies beyond the last breath.[19]

A metaphysical system is limited by horizons beyond which its initial framework cannot extend, simply because any such system is constructed from within a particular, necessarily limited, socio-linguistic framework. Metaphysical philosophers, Eastern and Western, start by establishing basic definitions for the elements of reality, then build up their worldview based on these dependently arisen definitions, mistaking them for unquestionable first principles. In fact, this is generally the approach we human beings take to arrive at any sort of viewpoint. In order to understand something, we break it into images based upon some background paradigm that is familiar to us, and then we use language to organize these images into known categories and depict the world accordingly. In this way, our own methods of understanding are not far different from the Abhidharma Buddhist philosophers of ancient India.

Such a schematic understanding of the world has its uses and its limited validity, based as it is upon human perception, thought, and judgment. With conventional truth, we fly airplanes and send space robots to Mars. When it comes to the quest for absolute truth, however, Nāgārjuna points out the futility of these common avenues of human knowing. He thus rejects as false any such human effort to grasp an absolute and de-

---

19. Heschel, *Man is Not Alone*, 8–9.

finitive picture of reality. For him, such a picture cannot exist, and so he would overturn all our most precious assumptions about truth and the nature of reality.

Nāgārjuna's equation of the two Middle Path themes of emptiness and dependent arising, and the consequent undermining of human viewpoints, were of immense importance to the subsequent development of Mahāyāna thinking, as indeed to our present endeavor in the philosophy of religions. Equally important, however, are Nāgārjuna's succinct comments about the two truths.

Two truths—ultimate and conventional

Middle Path philosophy moves on from its insight into emptiness to consider what that insight might mean for the human activities of thinking and judging. And so, the second major theme for the Middle Path is the discussion of two truths—ultimate truth and conventional truth. The insights that arise from this discussion can be extremely helpful when thinking about competing claims of truth from the many different religious traditions.

In the Christian West, thinkers and mystics were well aware that human words could not represent God, failing at every turn of discourse. So they, too, critiqued affirmative theology. They taught that because we do not know what terms like "good" or "eternal" mean when applied to God, we must proceed through a negative theology, unlearning all familiar meanings to abide in the silent wonder of not-knowing. But that negative theology does not serve the need for clear thinking and apologetics. Therefore, from at least the early Middle Ages, Western theological traditions tended to marginalize mysticism precisely because people felt the need to explicate the meaning of doctrine in clear, if analogical, terms. Silence could be left to the mystics, who enjoyed prayer and meditation. Besides, it was felt, if mystics were allowed to claim truth and reality in virtue of some silent and direct experience, then anybody could claim anything at all without fear of contradiction.

And so Western theologians added a third category. Besides the path of affirmation and the path of negation, they began to speak of the path of analogy. We could properly apply to God words whose meaning we knew from our own lives, but only by way of analogy, so that God was not good but super-good. This third path of analogy came to be termed the way of excellence—*via eminentioris* in Latin. Gradually, it shoved the negative thrust of mystic thought aside and achieved dominance in the development of Christian doctrine.

The Mahāyāna thinkers did not develop such a third step, but their two truths—conventional and ultimate—do parallel the Christian paths of affirmation and negation. Usually, these Buddhists remained content to teach the tensive balancing of the two truths, with a stress on the negations that liberate. If they had developed a third step, it might well have been called the way of humility—*via humilitatis*—for it would have consisted in reclaiming affirmation within its human and dependently arisen context. Let us see how they did approach the issue.

Ultimate truth, Middle Path philosophy tells us, is a truth beyond language. It is silent and ungraspable. If even the things of this world possess no inner essence that defines them, then clearly it is not possible to make absolute statements about something called the truth of ultimate meaning. The Sanskrit term for this ultimate truth means literally the final, or ultimate, meaning or aim.[20] Perhaps we can understand it as the truth that is the ultimate term or end point of all our questioning and all our thinking.[21]

Ultimate truth can serve as data for nothing at all. It is not a resource to which we might appeal for the verification or validation of anything.[22] Its being is silence. It enters into no argumentation. No knowing smiles or subtle appeals avail. It does not justify anything, nor does it lead to knowledge of anything. Yet, although ultimate truth cannot affirm anything, this is not a recommendation for a muddle-headed mysticism that would bypass thinking in favor of vague, untestable, direct experience. Ultimate meaning cannot trump the tasks of properly engaged theology or philosophy, which of necessity function verbally in the conventional world in light of clusters of dependently arisen experiences and insights.

20. In Sanskrit, *paramārtha*—*parama* meaning "final" or "ultimate" and *artha* signifying "meaning" or "aim."

21. Fredericks' tensive practice of friendship and comparative theology as acts of hope in his *Faith among Faiths*, 169–79, and O'Leary's focus on eschatology in his *Religious Pluralism*, 251–58, parallel such an understanding of ultimate truth. As does Lonergan's notion of God as the term of the unrestricted pure desire to understand.

22. This is the overarching point of Hakamaya's critique of Buddhist notions of Buddha Nature, the dhātuvāda he argues is a distortion. See his *Hihan bukkyō*.

The goal of the practitioner in Mahāyāna Buddhism is often stated to be direct, unmediated experience. However, the effect of such experience is to render the practitioner silent, bringing to a halt the mind's discriminations of insight and judgment. An experience of the ineffable is meant to tame the unruly mind, to break through its attachment to language as the carrier of all meaning. But then, when one returns to argument, or theology, or interfaith dialogue—or indeed to working out a philosophy of religious pluralism—no direct line leads from the silent truth of direct experience to enlightened verbalization. On these occasions, one is bounced willy-nilly back into ordinary and quite human realms of verbal expression, set free to work within and through a cultural context, but conscious of the limits of what language is able to say and in no way privileged in the saying.

And so, while meditation and direct experience are indeed central to Mahāyāna religious practice, Mahāyāna thinkers make little attempt to translate into words the practitioner's inexpressible experience of the numinous. That experience lies within the realm of ultimate truth. A religious practitioner may have been transformed by awakening, but there is no linear way to articulate that awakening in words.

Ordinarily, we must operate in the realm of a different kind of truth—one that is grounded in the world and bounded by its conventions. This is truth that we *can* express in language and adjudicate by normal and recognized rules of reasoning. Here, we are thrown back upon the humble, human endeavor to attend, to think, and to speak. This is conventional truth, and it remains human. [23] It is limited by the supply of images that our sense experiences provide, and by the occurrence of insight into those images. Conventional truth is a verbal truth. It is enunciated by the converted mind in particular circumstances.

Middle Path philosophers, as we have seen above, identify emptiness with dependent arising. Emptiness and dependent arising are offered as two different ways to describe the same thing—the essence-free being of all things, which arise in mutual dependence. These are two different ways to account for the phenomena of this world, and they are inextricably linked one to the other. By contrast, the two truths are *never* to be equated or identified one with the other. The silent truth of ultimate meaning and

23. In the classical Buddhist language of Sanskrit, this truth of worldly convention is called *saṃvṛti-satya*, for it is truth (*satya*) that functions in terms of agreed-upon conventions and, as such, it is clothed (*saṃvṛti*) in language.

the verbal truth of worldly convention are completely and utterly separate and different from one another. There can be no link between them.

And yet, both truths are empty: Ultimate truth has no identifiable essence and no conditions that might lead to its identification. Conventional truth is equally empty, for it is based on judgments that we have drawn from dependently arisen images and insights, which are ever subject to change and to new experience. Since conventional truths depend upon their cultures of origin both for images and for the terms in which those images are expressed, these truths can never claim to be absolute or universal. The truth of worldly convention can never rise above its own conditionality. For that reason, no conventional truth—the only kind of truth that we human beings can put into words—can claim to be normative once and for all, for all people.

This analysis of truth is highly critical of human knowing. It puts all human affirmations and assertions and claims of knowledge under scrutiny, and it collapses every one, including the claims of religious doctrine. St. Paul expressed this insight very well in 1 Corinthians 8:1b–3: "Knowledge puffs up, but love builds up. Anyone who claims to know something does not yet have the necessary knowledge; but anyone who loves God is known by him." This rejection of puffed-up knowledge is not a form of nihilism. Indeed, Middle Path thinkers criticize those who would wrongly identify the absence of essence as pure nothingness. Candrakīrti writes:

> If one imagines that, just because the entire realm of things is devoid of essence, it does not exist in any sense, then a serious heresy has taken hold of him.[24]

This point is crucial to understanding the relationship between the two truths. Far from depicting a world of meaninglessness and nihility, emptiness describes a world that is replete with dependently arisen meaning and truth, already replete yet unrecognized.[25]

The two truths offer us a paradigm for recognizing that conventional truths—the truths of Christianity, Buddhism, Islam, Judaism—can be meaningful and valid without needing to claim that their revelations

---

24. Candrakīrti, *Lucid Exposition*, 233.

25. See in Nishitani, *Religion and Nothingness*, his essay, "What is Religion?" 1–45, and van Bragt's "Translator's Introduction," xxiii–xlii. For the fullest and most insightful treatment of Nishitani and the Kyoto School, see Heisig, *Philosophers of Nothingness*.

are absolute or final. The validity and the meaning of conventional truths are always grounded in the conventional world where we live, without reference to any universally valid truth or principle. Even assertions that are regarded as revealed and inspired must always be judged within the world, for any truth that we can articulate in words—that is, conventional truth—will of necessity depend upon the particular language and images available in its own cultural context.[26]

Even Nāgārjuna's doctrine of emptiness must be seen as expressing only a conventional truth. Precisely because it is a doctrine taught verbally and expressed philosophically, it *cannot* be ultimate truth. As rational argument, Nāgārjuna's doctrine resides in the realm of conventional truth, with no appeal to any independent reality "out there" that it might claim to be ultimately true.

Nāgārjuna understands that the words he employs are themselves dependently arisen, taking their meaning from within particular worldly and conventional contexts. He does not, like those he critiques, presuppose that his own words correspond to self-existent, independent essences. The emptiness critique stands counter to any naïve realism that would assume words are capable of capturing reality. It is meant to cure our overweening confidence that we possess "the truth." It critiques those who would create viewpoints out of conventional language and images and then assert that those viewpoints possess ultimate and universal validity.

The aim of the philosophy of emptiness is to evaluate and to criticize human methods of perceiving, understanding, and knowing reality. Its equation of emptiness with dependent arising offers us an approach toward silent awakening to ultimate truth. It also encourages a critical awareness of how we human beings make true affirmations and negations, of the way in which we can arrive at conventional truth in this world—conventionally. In the end, emptiness points to truth by weaning us from our conviction

---

26. This is why, so it would seem, Ratzinger (Pope Benedict XVI) in his *Truth and Tolerance*, 66–71, argues that Christianity is itself a culture, and why he longs to restore a Christian culture to the West. It is why Islamic cultures sometimes enforce the harsh laws that no Muslim may ever convert to another faith. Clearly the Pope realizes the underlying support Christian culture and philosophy have provided for the developments of Christian doctrine and history. I think the Muslim stricture of narrow-minded mullahs against conversions is not only irrational but even silly, and that Pope Benedict will be disappointed in his efforts to maintain a Christian culture in the West. It would be better to ground our faith within our vernacular traditions in a truly cosmopolitan and multifaith world.

that we have the ability to articulate, and thereby to contain or possess, any absolute truth—even in the doctrines of our faith.

Although one might suspect that Nāgārjuna's discussion of two truths would argue against faith and practice, its apparent skepticism actually works in support of the practice of the spiritual path. Indeed, the teachers of the Middle Path demand that—if we wish to embark upon the path and pass from worldly convention to ultimate meaning—we must relinquish the self and all the elements of this world as empty and essence-free. We must also abandon the notion of any final goal or destination as the end point of the path. In synergistic tension, we seek and pray as practitioners of a middle path that threads its way through the complex interactions between faith and culture. It is not a ladder or a highway from here to there, for every end point is emptied, as is every point of beginning. In other words: Out with metaphysics and overviews! In with human belief, thinking, and acting![27]

Thus, the teaching of the two truths demonstrates that the meaning of any one doctrine or symbol of a religion can be determined only within the social and historical context wherein it plays a part. The only absolute truth is that of "no truth." In the end—in awareness of the two truths—we understand that we can never attain to a final or independent viewpoint. In the everyday world, any truth that can be established is of necessity dependent upon the criteria of our experience and reasoning. That experience may indeed be revelatory, and the reasoning may be theologically sound, but there is no direct, linear pathway from this everyday, conventional truth to the ultimate. Christians, too, catch only a glimpse—Moses-like—of the "backside" of a departing God; no one can see God and live.

The truth of faith liberated from the absolute

The idea that the truth we seek can never be captured as absolute is indeed hard to swallow. It would seem that the search for absolute truth is a fundamental human goal. We remember theologian Karl Rahner's claim that one cannot commit to a faith unless it is a matter of something absolute.

---

27. David Loy works out the implications of emptiness for a Buddhist psychology and a Buddhist social theory. The pattern is that of Mahāyāna philosophy, drawing it beyond its traditional textual sources into engagement in modern thought. See Loy, *Lack and Transcendence*, and *Great Awakening*.

And yet here, Nāgārjuna tells us, we are doomed to fail! But the Middle Path is not a road leading to failure and bleak skepticism.

In fact, the philosophy of the two truths provides a rich and useful paradigm for understanding how mystical and silent awareness does find expression in the religious traditions—that is, how in the everyday world of mediated meaning and verbal expression, we do seek and point to the ends of the cosmos of all our meanings. Human beings of every culture and tradition have always employed conventional modes of perception, language, reason, conceptualization, myth, and ritual to express their efforts to understand the world, to see into reality, and to know truth. They have done so in the context of their conventional and actual lives, listening to the silent voice of revelation and then clothing that revelation in terms known and understood by actual people.

Divine or numinous experience is a central aspect of all religion. "Ultimate meaning" is the term Buddhists use to refer to this silent, mystic, and unmediated awareness. They regard this mystic awareness as equivalent to reaching the state they call *nirvāna*, or cessation. In this state, the practitioner has relinquished any conception of selfhood and, the Middle Path thinkers tell us, is therefore able to see—that is, to experience—reality "as it is." All the usual modes of perception and all thought processes are brought to a halt so that the awakening practitioner is able to let "the myriad things come forth and experience themselves." In Christian terms, this is abandoning oneself to the will of God and experiencing the world in all its godly silence and all its worldly ambiguity.[28]

In Buddhist thinking, mystical awareness enables one to see the everyday world from a selfless perspective but it is not itself that seeing. In a characteristic Mahāyāna paradoxical turnabout, transcending the everyday world into cessation entails coming back to that same everyday world and seeing it from ever-new perspectives, all of which are constructs. Transcending the world, then, results in recognizing the world as dependently arisen—the understanding that whatever happens in that world happens in virtue of the multifaceted gift that we call our life. The life to which one awakens is not some other life, but *this* life, which has been present in its transient fullness all along.

The quest for a transcendent, ultimate meaning is a quest to see the reality of the very world that has been transcended. This is why Mahāyāna

28. Dōgen, "Actualizing the Fundamental Point," 69.

teaches that "nirvāna is saṃsāra" (final cessation = worldly suffering), for awakening is attested not by some supernatural addition to one's life[29] but rather by one's new ability to perceive the everyday conventional world "just as it is," in all its dependently arisen historicity. Nothing in the world has actually been transcended, but our minds have been profoundly altered and our sight regained. In the language of Christian faith, we now understand that all that happens arises from the will of God, not as divine manager or controller, but as that which lies beyond all human will. Even the crucifixion of the Lord Jesus was the outflow of the many actions then performed. His obedience to the Father's will signifies his total immersion in the way things were then, and the way they are now.

For Middle Path commentator Candrakīrti, emptiness—by its darkening of all approaches—directs one back toward conventional truth. Yet it is not as if one has reached a dead-end sign and is now forced to retrace one's steps in grim resignation along the same old tired and jejune road. Rather, one has experienced wisdom apart from all mediating structures and all cultures, and now realizes—precisely because that experience of wisdom is unmediated by human language or culture—that it can serve no role at all as data for further reflection. Emptiness is purely deconstructive and, as such, it cannot by itself establish any meaningful truth claim.

In order to affirm anything, conventional truth—whether it is expressed in terms of the deconstructive doctrine of emptiness or in terms of the constructive doctrine of wisdom—must always refer to the conventional world itself. It is for this reason that the two truths are absolutely separate, absolutely unrelated one to the other. When a conventional truth is content to be simply conventional, it reflects a humble awareness of the emptiness of ultimate meaning but it does not and cannot represent that ultimate meaning directly. It is more of an echo sounding off a distant wall than a mirroring of deep experience, more of a rebound back to a realm of mediated, earth-bound meaning than a manifestation of the otherness of ultimate meaning.

When a thinker enunciates conventional truth in awareness of emptiness and appropriates ever-new meanings and new insights into mediated truth, that regained understanding "can only be described as a

---

29. Rahner, *Nature and Grace*, 35, the main point of the essay being that pure nature is no more than an abstract category without actual existence, for lived lives are already bathed in grace.

resurrection, a restoration,"[30] precisely because the thinker is now more attentive to experience than before, and more intelligent in understanding. In being resurrected, however, conventional truth is not elevated to a higher plane. It is "lowered" to the level of simple convention, enmeshed profoundly in the world in which we actually live. Importantly, however, conventional truth is not being established for the first time, as something new. It is the "resurrection" of a world that was already there to begin with. Awakening, then, entails seeing the conventional everyday world in a new way, as "merely" conventional.

Nor does the notion of return to a world that was present from the beginning signify the recovery of some pristine condition, some "pure" state that existed prior to all language and all discrimination. It means instead that the otherness of ultimate meaning does not impinge upon worldly and conventional modes of thought and awareness. The conventional world continues just as it is, operating solely in terms of worldly and conventional principles.[31] Awareness of ultimate meaning does not impose any sort of ultimately valid logic or logos from above, but simply and merely allows the human world of mediated meaning to function as authentically human.

The Word really becomes enfleshed and subject to conventional suffering and worldly action. The Word incarnate who is Christ is not a double-tiered person, but the same divine ultimate God and the same human and conventional enfleshment. Emptiness is not an attack upon the functioning of conventional reason and logic in the conventional world. It is an attack on the presumption that conventional means can ever be adequate to ascertain some universal truth that might exist outside conventional frameworks. Likewise it affirms the conventional words we do use to witness and to preach within this world and its history.

There is more to this Mahāyāna philosophy of the two truths than exhortations to be silent and still. Worldly truth does exist, and it is important. As Nāgārjuna states:

> Those who do not understand
> The distinction drawn between these two truths
> Do not understand
> The Buddha's profound truth.

30. Nagao, *Foundational Standpoint*, 103.
31. Ibid., 104.

Without a foundation in the conventional truth
The significance of the ultimate cannot be taught.
Without understanding the significance of the ultimate
Liberation is not achieved.[32]

If we comprehend that ultimate meaning is completely and entirely other and apart from our human world, we come to the realization that no conventional worldly truth—even the tenets of our own cherished religious tradition—can ever be considered as absolute. At the same time, unless we are grounded in conventional truth, we will never understand or practice the path to wisdom.

With this understanding of the two truths, we are restored to our humanness. We give up overblown claims that assume our ability to grasp absolute reality. Then we can reclaim the conventional truth of our traditions as completely and fully human. We do not need to reject the existence of propositional, right-or-wrong truth, but we do clarify its status. Propositional truth can be robustly true in a worldly context, but it can never lay claim to ultimate validity. In other words, the truth of our faith may always be embraced as true enough to die for, but never asserted as true enough to kill for.

This limitation is neither negative nor pessimistic. Instead, it reclaims a new, dynamic notion of how we human beings may seek truth—through attentiveness to experience, understanding of that experience, and intelligent judgment of the validity of ideas and insights derived from that experience. It allows truth to live in its human environment and—importantly—to adapt itself to varying occasions and needs within each culture and context of meaning.

Certainly there is something positive to be gained when our quest for truth is liberated from aspirations to the absolute. We can now recognize our own limitations, and "it is only in recognition of our ignorance that we are capable of understanding truth, only in an awareness of our ugliness and sin that we ascend to beauty and goodness."[33] When we accept our humanity and its limitations, we are able to enunciate verbal truths with the recognition that they are "conventional-only," as the Mahāyānists say. We are empowered to reject the false and to hold on to the true, not because what is "true" takes its validity from some universal law or prin-

---

32. Nāgārjuna, *Stanzas on the Middle*, 24:9–10; Garfield, *Fundamental Wisdom*, 298.
33. Nagao, *Foundational Standpoint*, 46.

ciple above and beyond the world—and most definitely not because it is rooted in some mystic experience—but because its truth is rooted in the world itself.

YOGĀCĀRA'S ANALYSIS OF THE MIND OF FAITH

Nagging questions about emptiness

French scholar Jacques May describes the philosophy of the Middle Path as "a discourse on the spirit." It leads—not to overarching, absolute statements about truth or detailed pictures of reality—but rather to an emptying of the spirit, an abandonment of all attachment.[34] The appeal of this Middle Path and its doctrine of emptiness is perhaps similar to the attraction some Christians find in the writings of St. John of the Cross or Nicholas of Cusa, mystics who define God by what God is *not* and who taste God in the "cloud of unknowing."

But the Middle Path teachings on emptiness left a trail of many questions and difficulties. There was the matter of Buddhism's traditional teaching on *karma*—past actions that bring about suffering in the present. Middle Path thinkers asserted that even karma is empty, that this world of suffering is the very same as the cessation of suffering. But whether or not karma is called empty, people do continue to act in habitual patterns that serve their own self-interest, to the detriment of others around them. Empty or not, the dynamic of karma continues in a never-ending cycle—human actions resulting in anger, violence, and suffering, in turn eliciting further actions producing the very same ugly results. How does emptiness explain all this?

Furthermore, the very territory of emptiness is a precarious and disorienting place. We would prefer to be surrounded and supported by a visible circle of family and friends. We want clear and present sustenance and shelter. Even the most reclusive refugee from this world of sorrow and delusion sometimes needs a bit of solid food. It seems obvious to most people that this is indeed a material world, but the Middle Path persists in maintaining that all things, all ideas, all persons, are radically transient—empty of any enduring essence that we can lean upon.

At gut level, we know very well that our ever-shifting, ever-changing lives and worlds are precarious and transient. The glorious, fiery foliage of

---

34. May, *Candrakīrti*, 15.

Vermont's autumn turns to brown, and gives way in turn to the black and white of winter. Sickness forces us to change our plans. Death snatches away our loved ones. We know these things. But it is right here that we live, right here that we act and interact. And sometimes people find that the Middle Path's insistent denial of a solid substance in the reality surrounding us is just too much to bear, too rarefied, too sour to the taste. Buddhist texts tell of practitioners who, upon hearing the demands of emptiness, fell into utter dejection and despair at ever becoming so pure in spirit, so detached.[35]

This despairing response to emptiness called forth another group of texts—the *Tathāgatagarbha* scriptures and their commentaries—which softened and indeed countered the doctrine of emptiness. These teachings declared that, although *delusions* are most certainly empty, the one true seed[36] of awakening[37] is not at all empty; it is pure, undefiled, and—reassuringly—eternal and immutable.[38] In this view, we are all really enlightened beings (*buddhas*), or at least potentially so. For we possess Buddha Nature.

This argument among Buddhist philosophers—the Middle Path proponents of emptiness on the one hand and the advocates of Buddha Nature (our true and very real potential for awakening) on the other—seesawed back and forth, over and over, without any prospect of conclusion. But in debates like this over religious views, whatever one side asserts as clear and decisive reasoning, the other side generally dismisses as either utterly childish teaching or just obvious rubbish.

In the political realm, one may perhaps see that the other side in a debate does have its points and so proceed to negotiate—a little for you, a little for me. Politics after all is the art of the possible. Not so with religious doctrine—these arguments tend to go on and on. To compromise in religious controversy, in fact, is to invite charges of betraying the tradition, or at the very least, watering it down. (How can you call yourself faithful Christians true to church teaching and tradition if you accept divorce? Ordain women clergy? Welcome homosexuals into the community and bless their relationships with one another?) In truth, it is not doctrine that

35. Takasaki, *Study of the Ratnagotravibhāga*, 305–6.

36. Or "womb"; Sanskrit, *garbha*.

37. Tathāgata, a title for the Buddha, meaning literally the "Thus (*tathā*) Gone One (*gata*)"—the one who has gone to awakening.

38. Wayman, *Lion's Roar*, 99.

usually gets watered down, but the rich soil of the arid mind that refuses to become fertile soil to receive the rain of doctrine that allows the seeds scattered by the sower to germinate and grow.

Distant in time and culture as it is, the Buddhist dispute described here has great relevance to our contemporary situation. Like many self-assured religious viewpoints that are popular today, the Indian Buddha Nature texts offered simple, reassuring, and pastoral teachings—"answers to life's persistent questions," as Garrison Keillor would have it. Answers—Who *doesn't* long for simple answers to the questions that bother us so much in this perplexing world? Nevertheless, the Middle Path thinkers persist in denying that there is any such thing as an absolutely true answer. They tell us that language itself, and anything that is affirmed in words, is empty, that it has no solid substance whatsoever.

Moreover, they point out, absolute statements have a tendency to fossilize and actually prevent practitioners from experiencing anything very significant at all. If the creeds of our tradition only fossilize and occlude the gospel, of what use is that tradition? Furthermore, if our very scriptures emerge as they do from ancient cultures and depend on images and insights that have long since lost their meaning for us, then what use are they to modern people trained to think critically? On the other hand, if religious teachings are indeed empty, then how can we commit our lives to faith traditions that are language-formed and language-expressed? When we engage in the study of our own and other faiths, are we then just studying archaic and irrelevant artifacts? Can we remain the rational children of the Enlightenment, which in this culture we clearly are, and still confess and practice our faith tradition wholeheartedly?

Practitioners of introspection

The Yogācāra school of Buddhist philosophy arose in part in response to controversies over opposing truth claims among the various Buddhist schools of thought. *The Scripture on the Explication of Underlying Meaning*, one of Yogācāra's earliest texts, opens with a vivid description of philosophical combat between proponents of different schools. The participants are depicted as clinging tenaciously to their own verbal descriptions of reality: "confronting one another and arguing fiercely, emitting barbed, pointed, captious, angry, vicious comments, without any hope of ever reaching a definitive conclusion."[39]

This may sound like the exchange of political rhetoric in twenty-first-century red and blue America, but the scene depicted is a debate over religious truth taking place in second-century India.[40] In either situation, the question is the same: How on earth can we determine which arguments are valid and which are not? The Yogācārins concluded that this kind of quandary can only be solved by looking inward, by analyzing the mental processes whereby we think and reach conclusions: How do we think? How do we judge? How do we understand? The discoveries that they made by looking into the human mind can be quite useful in our search for an effective philosophy of religious pluralism.

Yoga in the word Yogācāra refers to the practice of meditation—or perhaps here we could use the word "introspection." *Cāra* means "practitioner." The Yogācāra thinkers[41]—practitioners of introspection—looked inward to develop a philosophy of mind that could address the troubling issue of opposing truth claims. They carefully analyzed the operations of the mind that is deluded, and also the operations of the mind that understands. And they considered how the one might be converted to the other.

The Yogācāra philosophy of mind is a "critical" philosophy, because it focuses not simply on things out there in the world that are objects of human attempts to understand, but also—and most importantly—it attends to and analyzes the consciousness that seeks to understand. To become so aware of our own thinking process is not a particularly easy or natural thing for human beings to do. German philosopher Immanuel Kant, who

39. Keenan, *Scripture on the Explication,* 14–15.

40. The situation was complex: Yogācāra followed upon and was called forth from the Mādhyamika refutation of the conceptual realism of Abhidharma, whose systematic theoreticians contended that well-analyzed ideas correspond to actual essences. Meanwhile, the Buddha Nature doctrine of the Tathāgatagarbha teachers began to appeal to practitioners. All of these viewpoints were in contention in second-century India. Eventually, Yogācāra thought together with Mādhyamika laid the basis for subsequent Mahāyāna thinking. Still, the Tathāgatagarbha traditions, which in India focused upon practical spiritual teaching, provided a major theme in the doctrinal elaboration of the Chinese and Japanese schools of Buddhism, perhaps because of their consonance with the Taoist notion of our *original* nature.

41. Asaṅga, Vasubandhu, Sthiramati, Dharmapāla, and Hsüan-tsang, as well as the later epistemologists (*Pramāṇavāda*), Dignāga in China, and Dharmakīrti, who was transmitted only to Tibet.

lived in the 1700s, is generally considered to be the first to develop such a critical philosophy in the West. He sought to critique and clarify the implicit structures and forms of consciousness that are necessary for all understanding. In its time and place, Kantian philosophy was regarded as radical and revolutionary. It had a major influence on subsequent European thought.[42] But 1500 years before Immanuel Kant philosophized in Europe, Buddhist Yogācāra masters in India looked inward to study the structure and operations of the mind, and they developed their own critical understanding of human consciousness. An important difference between Kant and the Yogācārins is that Kant saw this analysis of the processes of mind as strictly a philosophical matter. For the Yogācāra thinkers, on the other hand, it had immense spiritual import, with crucial bearing on the issue of truth and conversion to emptiness.

Perhaps it came more naturally for Yogācāra philosophers than for Western thinkers to look inward, for they were formed and supported by their Buddhist culture and its long history of practicing meditation and concentration. Moreover, they accepted the experiences engendered by those contemplative practices not only as valid but also as supremely important. Most Western thinkers, by contrast, have dismissed any insights derived from meditation as epiphenomenal and insignificant. When the Yogācārins came to philosophize, they stepped back from their meditations, aware of insights they had been granted in those states, and attended to their mental operations. In this manner they came to understand how the human mind generates delusion, and how it may turn toward truth and wisdom.

How do we know? And how can we be sure that we know? Yogācārins ask these questions in order to ascertain the structure and operation of their own minds, and to come to terms with the ways in which human minds function properly or mistakenly. All with the end purpose, not of negating faith traditions, but of explicating them richly and confidently. As they sought to experience experiencing, think about thinking, understand understanding, and judge judgment, they remained within their

---

42. Kant led A.K. Chatterjee, in his *Yogācāra Idealism* to adopt his approach in interpreting Yogācāra, for Kant critiqued pure reason as reaching only to phenomena, and practical reason as embodying the conventional morality that we need to live. Kant is reported to have been rapt in wonder and awe at the starry sky above him and the moral law within him. Not many would follow Chatterjee's exposition of Yogācāra, but most follow his placement of Yogācāra as a critical philosophy of mind.

confessed faith context, for to them all is beside the point unless one practices the path.

In considering the nature of the mind that knows and how it knows, the Yogācāra thinkers wished to learn how the mind could reach a sure refuge for doctrine. After all, one of the Three Jewels of Buddhism is the Jewel of Doctrine.[43] It would not do for them simply to jettison all words, and languages, and views, just as it would not do to cling to them in self-content. So the Yogācārins sought to develop a method by which to interpret doctrine and to adjudicate truth claims. And because the numerous scriptures of the different Buddhist schools enunciated many truths, they needed a method for thinking critically about scripture and tradition.

The Yogācāra thinkers adopted the twin Middle Path concepts of emptiness and dependent arising as tools in their analysis of the mind. Applying these ideas to the realm of human consciousness, they devised a description of the mental operations by which human beings approach truth. Importantly for our purposes in developing a philosophy of religions, the Yogācārins' analysis bears upon questions of how religious conversion takes place, how doctrine is interpreted, and how we read and understand truth in the sacred writings of the traditions.

Employing the concept of emptiness, they affirm that beings have no supporting essence that might be imagined and grasped as corresponding to something that is essentially and objectively real. Indeed, they reject all forms of naïve realism—the view that we can know merely by taking a look at something. But this does not mean that the Yogācārins reject any possibility of valid and insightful thinking about the world. In fact, they embrace the notion of dependent arising as applied to the operations and activities of the mind and teach that the very genesis of meaning itself is dependently arisen.

The Middle Path notion of dependent arising is here brought to bear upon conscious interiority. The assumption of a simple subject-object dichotomy is negated. Mind comes to be and falls away in dependence upon its own other-dependent structure. All ideas and judgments depend upon how we sense the world, how we perceive what we sense, how we gain insight, and how we draw conclusions from our insights—within different cultures, different countries, and different states of practice. The Yogācāra analysis extends then to how we can distinguish between differences in

---

43. The "Three Jewels of Buddhism" are said to be the Buddha, the Dharma (teaching, or doctrine), and the Saṅgha (the religious community).

thinking and judgment that are generated because of different dependently arisen contexts on the one hand, and on the other, differences that are generated simply by error and delusion.

Becoming conscious of consciousness

Usually, and for most of our lives, we are not required to attend to attending, to think about thinking. We just *are* conscious, and we attend to whatever catches our attention. That is well enough for most of the tasks we need to execute: buying a car, or searching for the best prices for heating oil and pork chops. But how to treat questions of where we come from, who we are, and where we go? There are no entries in the yellow pages, anybody's yellow pages, for that. Often, in our very human preference for a commonsense and reassuring perspective, we are content to believe in the real reality of the Buddha within, or the encompassing and protective presence of our God, to live good and productive lives, and to die in some peace. And, in actual fact, a person who authentically does that is well worthy of our deep respect and admiration.

Indeed, issues about emptiness do not arise in the minds of many of us, and where in the West they do, they often arise in contexts that are decidedly anti-religious. Relativists and deconstructionists tell us that all ideas and all claims trace back and forth in endless chains of intellectual DNA helixes, and nobody is even trying to decipher that genome. But we in the West do have our mystic traditions that encourage us to look within. But these traditions do not focus on the mind and its activities, and thus cannot offer philosophical insights that would aid us to ground our faith and practice. They are vernacular mystic traditions, and they silence our favored vernacular traditions.

We can practice our faith under the tutelage of wise teachers and guides, but in the event that those very guides become suspect, contradicting one another or losing their credibility, we may be forced to turn inward, to develop our own theory of how we know. We will have to identify, in the context of our own experience and thinking, what meaning is and how we come to it.

"We are led by mind," the early Buddhist scripture says,[44] by our grasp of our personal history and culture, but the issue is more than personal.

---

44. See verse 1 of any of the many translations of the *Dharmapāda*, which is perhaps the earliest Buddhist text.

In a world of many traditions, it is crucial that we look inward, that we become practitioners of introspection. We today are aware of the beauty of other traditions and their obvious effectiveness for their many followers. This awareness pushes us back into our own minds, to learn and claim who *we* have become over our history, and how we might affirm all that entails, while at the same time learning to cherish and respect brothers and sisters of other faiths around the globe.

But turning our attention inward is not easy. Which is why these Yogācāra people call themselves *practitioners* of yoga, of yogic meditation. We may begin our attempt to look inward just with stillness and quiet, counting the breaths, in and out, calming the glut of electrical impulses within our minds, perhaps fasting to align blood glucose levels in our circulatory systems, and becoming aware of our bodies in their gifted functioning. Calmed somewhat then, we will begin to notice the great cinematic phantasmagoria of images that flit from one frame to the next, moment to moment. And we may become aware of how often we simply assume—without carefully attending to anything—that the images before us represent our world just as it is.

This is a good way to begin to become conscious of consciousness, for the more one attends to these images and questions them, the more one realizes that many or most of them are images we have simply accepted unthinkingly from our families, and teachers, and cultures. The story is told of a woman who always cut off the ends of a ham before putting it in the oven to bake. One day her inquisitive young daughter asks, "Mommy, why do you always do that?" The mother answers, "Well, I'm not really sure. My mother always did it that way, so that's just how I learned to fix ham." The little girl, her mind not yet closed by family tradition, runs straight upstairs to her grandmother and asks, "Grandma, *why* did you always cut the ends of the ham off before you baked it?" "Well, dear," the grandmother replies, "as I recall, my pan was too small to fit the whole thing in!" Common sense is replete with common nonsense.

Images do not guarantee truth. One day, behind St. Eddie's dormitory at St. Charles Seminary on the margins of the city of Philadelphia, I watched an immense insect, much larger than a common housefly, attack a large bee and actually carry it away. I saw it all very clearly, and seeing is believing, is it not? Some years later in a Chinese class at the University of Pennsylvania, my professor Derk Bodde was talking about cicadas in Chinese literature. He noted that we also had many cicadas in the Philadelphia area, and as he described them, I realized that the large "fly" I had once seen attacking a bee was actually a cicada. He went on to say, however, that cicadas are so gentle that one can pick them up and pet their silky wings. But, I told him, I saw one attack a big bee and even fly away with it. He frowned, thought a moment or two, and then re-interpreted what I had seen: There are, he explained, large bees that attack and eat cicadas, and my cicada was no doubt attempting to flee the clutches of the bee! Seeing might sometimes be believing, but it is not necessarily understanding. Do not always trust your eyes.

Questioning, all questioning—even irreverent and embarrassing questioning—is always the beginning of understanding. Deep and simple questions: Who is God? Why is God so obviously not in charge of very much? Was Jesus *really* like other male human beings? In every way? Such questions get to the heart of issues: What is ultimate? Are we at all cared for? Is Jesus truly human? Too often questions like these are discouraged or dismissed as too simple, already covered, quite clearly explained in the book if you would but look it up, or simply stupid. But the persistent—indeed the stubborn—do not give up; they merely postpone their puzzlements. Dwell in the question, imagine its contours, and raise parallel questions. Become aware of the activity of questioning. Go beyond school learning—which always by its institutional nature provides answers for questions someone else thinks you should have asked but perhaps have not, for you have other, different questions.

Some mental states are easy to identify. We all know what it is to think, to ponder. Indeed, cognitive theory can even depict a person thinking, eyes cast down like Rodin's "The Thinker." And we recognize what it is to get the point, to have that light bulb go off in our minds and to exclaim in triumph like Archimedes, running naked through the streets of Syracuse because he had finally figured out how to determine whether the king's crown was really pure gold.[45] Insights into images do occur. A critical analysis of mind takes as the ground of meaning such experiences of perceiving things in error and then thinking through to truth. It seeks to understand how all the operations of mind interrelate, how images function, where bright ideas come from, and how then one can judge this or that to be true.

45. Lonergan, *Insight*, 27–31.

Any attempt to treat world religions would do well to attend to the structure of mind, for this does, as Catholic theologian Bernard Lonergan claims, remain invariant through all cultures and lands. Our minds function by experiencing sensed objects, perceiving their contours, gaining or not gaining insight into those perceptions, and judging insights to be true or not.[46] Nobody ever claims that they have no experience, do not gain insight, never make reasonable judgments, or that they think it unimportant to follow the path of their respective faiths. Lonergan had to think very hard and very long to write his tome on *Insight* and to explicate the structure and functioning of the mind.[47] So did the Yogācārins centuries earlier.

The mind as the very model of dependent arising

The Yogācāra thinkers[48] based their analysis of the human mind upon an understanding of emptiness and dependent arising. Their goal in analyzing the structure and operations of the mind was to increase understanding of how we read and interpret scripture. In *The Scripture on the Explication of Underlying Meaning*, the foundational Yogācāra text, they spell out their insights.

This Yogācāra scripture explains that over time there have been "three turnings of the Wheel of Doctrine"—three ever-deepening stages

46. In place of the apoha theory of the Buddhist logicians, I prefer Lonergan, *Method in Theology*, 66–76, on judgment as that special case of insight that understands what all the relevant requirements are for a statement to be true, and whether in fact all are met.

47. Lonergan, "Cognitional Structure," 2.3. I am aware that in so constructing my presentation of Yogācāra philosophy I am following both the Chinese practice of ignoring the developments in Buddhist logic and epistemology that followed in India, and that I am here grafting the branches of a Western philosophy onto the trunk of Mahāyāna. I am encouraged in this syncretistic move by the Chinese, who did not translate very much of later Indian Buddhist logic and epistemology, apparently because they did not themselves understand it. On the other hand, perhaps such a small number of Indian Buddhist texts on logic and epistemology were translated into Chinese because it was quite apparent that they did not harmonize with the cultural and philosophical traditions of China—K'ung-sun Lun, and in particular Chuang Tzu's abandonment of logic for experience and immediacy. China had a millennium of philosophy by the time these Indian Buddhists were trying to explicate their logic, and much of Chinese early philosophy takes direct aim at the surety of language and discriminative thinking. Furthermore, in the absence of a body of mutually referring Buddhist texts on logic and epistemology (the greatest of these thinkers, Dharmakīrti, was never translated at all) modern scholars have not been able to develop concordances and dictionaries of this vocabulary that might prosper such investigations.

48. Principally Asaṅga and Vasubandhu.

of doctrine taught by the Buddha in the *sūtras*, the Buddhist scriptures. The first turning of the Wheel of Doctrine included the initial teachings of the Buddha as presented in early Indian and Chinese texts.[49] The second turning of the Wheel taught the emptiness of all things. Clearly, this refers to the *New Perfection of Wisdom Scriptures*, which expounded emptiness and dependent arising, and the scriptures of Middle Path philosophy. As we have seen, the latter are those challenging teachings that detach the self from any firm and comfortable base, for all is empty of solid essence and arises in dependence on a host of factors.

This Yogācāra text explains that the third turning of the Wheel, the last of the progressively deeper teachings offered by the Buddha, is in fact identical in its teaching content to the second. The only difference between the two is that the third turning or teaching—the Yogācāra—does what the Middle Path neglected to do: It explains how karma works, clarifies the claims about emptiness and dependent arising, and demonstrates how these concepts apply to the human mind. *The Explication of Underlying Meaning* asserts that the second turning of the Wheel—the Middle Path—did not spell out *why* all viewpoints are to be rejected as empty. Nor did it clearly explain how it is that the human mind in some cases weaves delusion while in other cases it embraces awakening. Because of these crucial omissions, the Middle Path teachings had continued to be an object of controversy and criticism.

Only the third turning of the Wheel—the Yogācāra teaching—is beyond controversy, for it is based upon a careful consideration of the mind and its operations. It shows how delusion and erroneous viewpoints are generated in the human mind, and how that same mind can instead turn toward awakening and the teaching of wisdom. This scripture presents Yogācāra teachings, not as superior, but rather as clarifying the "underlying meaning" the Middle Path scriptures and philosophy, the second turning of the Wheel. The Yogācāra thinkers focus upon "conscious interiority," that is, upon our awareness of our own minds, how they are structured, how they function.

And the way in which the human mind operates, the Yogācārins tell us, is a model of the dependent arising first described by the Middle Path: The mind functions by means of a multitude of factors that come into being in dependence upon one another. The Yogācārins enumerate eight

49. The Pali Canon and the Chinese Āgamas, plus the Abhidharma theory in its many systematic tractates.

factors that act together to influence human thinking: the five senses, perception, defiled thinking, and the latent "storehouse consciousness."

The storehouse consciousness is where karma comes into play, and it is the key to the genesis of delusion or—when converted—of wisdom. It contains the "seeds," or habitual thought patterns, that have accumulated over time as the result of our past actions and experiences. For good or for ill, these seeds continue unconsciously to influence our thoughts and actions into the present. In traditional Buddhist thinking, this influence may even carry over from a past life. The story is told of a famous Buddhist teacher who, quite unlike his colleagues, had a pronounced fondness for jewelry and fine clothing. The Buddha explained that those habits were a natural carryover from one of the man's previous lives, when he was a popular and alluring courtesan!

Previous lives aside, we can easily observe the influence within a single lifetime of past training or long habit: A scholar will get up in the morning, eat breakfast, and then spend hours at the desk or in the laboratory reading, researching, and writing about new ideas or discoveries. An artist may awaken to new visions of colors and shapes. A stockbroker, long focused on the market and its trends, will likely begin the day thinking how to make the most profitable trades for clients. A loan shark, on the other hand, may well wake up devising new schemes to bilk *his* clients. And so forth.

Our thinking can be defiled not only by karmic seeds from our storehouse consciousness, but also by our very common tendency to mistake images for insight and then chase after those images. The mind is not, as we might expect, an inner camera simply snapping pictures of objects out there, displaying them to us accurately, just as they are. That is delusion. What we perceive is the product of a mind that itself is the scene of constant interplay between the input of the five senses, their perceptions, defiled thinking, and all the influences unwittingly engendered by latent habits and tenacious errors stored up in the past but ever operative in the present. Yogācāra thinkers knew something about what Augustine called original sin—engendered simply by being born into the world.

Three patterns of thinking

This mind of ours, so structured, has three patterns in which it can function, the Yogācārins tell us. For the most part everywhere, people function in what they call the "imagined pattern," when they are not aware of the processes of their own minds, and are not engaged in the search for awakening. People generally live in the assumption that the images they perceive, by and in themselves, really offer something desirable to grasp after—or else something unwanted to push away—always from the perspective of a self that is falsely conceived to be real.

This is everyday delusion, the ordinary pattern by which the world works: the quest for money and power, the rage for revenge, the seven deadly sins of pride, envy, sloth, jealousy, avarice, lust, and anger—or, more concisely, the three poisons of greed, anger, and delusion. If I see a pot of gold, I want it and I take it; if later I lose it, I am angry. If a man sees a beautiful woman, he desires her; if she rejects him, he is hurt. This is called the imagined pattern because the images do *not* represent reality. They are constructs of our own perception and are in fact transient, ephemeral—like bubbles in a spring, like the son of a barren woman, or horns on a rabbit, as the Buddhists say.

The mind functioning in the imagined pattern is a lazy mind. It falls back on habitual attitudes, which were formed in the past and continue to distort human thinking. In this pattern, the mind fails to reflect upon or to ask any questions about the image it perceives and, failing thus to gain insight into that image, it follows its natural bent toward self-delusion. It does not bother to ask how we process the images in our world, the sounds that we hear, or the things that we see. It just accepts those images at face value.

Once I was in love with a beautiful French woman. She was so really real that I would with alacrity have given up all else to wed and live with her in Paris. But we never sat down to envisage a realistic future; we were simply love-struck, I perhaps more than she. She turned out, despite her younger age, to be more practical than I and to see how deluded my images of our Parisian life together were. Deluded in love. Later I met and married Linda, a young woman from Iowa. We share not only a deep love one for the other but also many common interests and a practical approach to our family life and work. We do not dwell in the Paris of my imagined delusions.

Another simple example of such an image might be my youthful sighting of a great grey "brain" quivering in the breeze in the middle of the highway leading up from the old Norfolk ferry in Delaware. The cars from the ferry had passed, and the scene was silent and surreal—a fearsome, giant brain blocking my path on an empty highway. My friend and I got out of the car and slowly, nervously approached the thing, with cinematic pictures of "The Blob" dancing in our heads. The closer we got, the more it looked like the inner grey matter of a brain, and the more we began to work ourselves into a shared state of apprehension. Inches away, it looked no different, and we began to imagine what a brain like that could do to us. The blob in the movie had been able to slither over the ground and engulf people. Finally, I reached out and lightly touched it, and the sinister object revealed itself to be the innards of some old mattresses that had fallen off a truck. It had quivered so strangely there in the moonlight, and only after I reached out—with great trepidation—to investigate it, to touch and attempt to identify it, did it once again regain its terrestrial nature. The images our senses perceive—especially in combination with stored memories of an old horror movie—can indeed mislead our minds.

But the mind does possess the ability to function validly and effectively. In the second, "other-dependent pattern" of consciousness, insight depends upon image but is not identical with it. Here, insight occurs into the meaning of the image. This becomes possible when the seeds in the storehouse consciousness have been eradicated through hearing the Buddha's teaching and practicing the path of concentrated meditation. Thinking then becomes undefiled, and the perception of sense experience wholesome. This happens, however, only with the conversion of consciousness—away from the delusion of imagined realities to the perfection of the wisdom of the Buddha. The conversion of consciousness enables us to reclaim the valid other-dependent pattern of perceiving, thinking, and judging.

Consciousness converted, we are now aware of our human mental structure, realizing that no element or level of consciousness or activity stands alone but instead operates always in dependence upon other mental activities. We are accordingly liberated from unconscious influences—of past actions, images, and ideas. We understand the interplay between sense perception and thinking, and are thus enabled to consider and question the image before us, which appears to be so very real. That image no longer simply validates itself; we question and ponder and seek insight into it. Once we gain that insight, we can then think clearly in the other-dependent pattern, in the realization that all images, all ideas, and indeed all languages, are historically and culturally conditioned.

This pattern of thinking can serve us well in seeking to form true ideas about other people's religious traditions. We are not, for example, to stop at superficial impressions of unfamiliar rites and practices; we are to take into account foreign origins and cultural and language differences. When we employ the other-dependent pattern of thinking, we are able both to regard and respect "the other" and to enunciate our own doctrine truly and effectively, even indeed (as the Buddhist scriptures teach) infallibly. The path so brought to speech may then be true and effective in leading practitioners of our tradition toward awakening and compassionate engagement in the world. Truth, though infallible, remains language-formed and culturally constructed. How else could we say anything?

But it does take work to transcend our usual imagined pattern of thinking and attain to the valid and effective other-dependent pattern of consciousness. It requires long meditation and critical thinking. Errors abound. I still doggedly maintain that during our honeymoon summer of 1972, my wife Linda and I sat on a swing in the gazebo at Jelly Mill Common just south of Burlington, Vermont. I assert this as fact still today, because I can see it so vividly in my mind. Alas, it has been proven to me by longtime Vermont residents (and reiterated by my wife) that this cannot have happened. Jelly Mill Common did not exist in 1972. It was built only some years later. The image I was—and remain—so sure about fails the tests of questioning and investigation, for it is a prerequisite that the place first had to exist before we could sit in its swing. I remain certain that we did so, and this certainty comes right out of the deluded imagined pattern of consciousness. It is a mistaken judgment—as my wife will attest.

The third pattern of conscious understanding in the Yogācāra analysis is called the "perfected pattern" of consciousness. This refers to Buddha awakening and the perfection of wisdom. This pattern functions only in the wisdom of silence, where all the seeds of the unconscious have been abandoned, and even sense perception and thinking have ceased. Here, one abides far from the imagined pattern of delusion and self-craving, in the silent awakening that is called cessation. But in the Mahāyāna tradition, although such silent awakening is indeed beyond all ideas and all judgment, one may not abide there. Emptiness, as the Middle Path so clearly teaches, entails dependent arising. The awakened one returns to the world of thinking and teaching, to engage in the conventional truth of the world of sentient beings.

Contemplating the truth of scripture and doctrine

Yogācāra philosophy laid a foundation for interpreting scripture and doctrine by attending to the nature of the consciousness that understands the scriptures and lives in the truth. Its analysis of the structure of the human mind and the interdependent nature of understanding shows how delusion may arise and thus, by reversal, how it may be abandoned. The Yogācāra description of the three patterns of thought demonstrates that the basic pattern of our conscious functioning is other-dependent—an interplay of many influences—and that it may swing either toward delusion or toward awakening and wisdom.

The Yogācāra thinkers, like all classical Buddhist thinkers, based themselves upon the scriptural tradition. They lived within their Buddhist culture and insisted that in order to attain conversion to wisdom it is necessary to hear and to ponder the scriptures. Indeed, Yogācāra philosopher Asvabhāva reported the Buddha as insisting that before one could understand the teachings, he must first read the entire, vast collection of the scriptures.[50] The scriptures are central. Even when the Buddhist teachers are introducing a new notion, as when Asaṅga is demonstrating the existence of the storehouse consciousness, they always claim that the concept has already been taught *implicitly* in earlier texts. The new is merely an interpretation of what has been present in the scriptural tradition all along.[51] And so all teachings are seen as grounded in the scriptures and their interpretation.

But one must not merely read the scriptures and categorize their teachings. Equally important is to *comprehend* the intention with which they were preached. Asvabhāva explains:

> Up until now, explanations of the meaning [of the scriptures] have not taken into consideration the intention of [their] author. But it is in taking into consideration that intention that one should explain the meaning of what has been declared.[52]

Today, it is out of vogue to consider the intent of the author in Western literary studies, including biblical studies. How, it is asked, can one ever be sure what the ancient writer had in mind? However, at least until the middle of the twentieth century, ascertaining the author's in-

50. Nagao, *Shōdaijōron*, commentary on 3.1.
51. Asaṅga, *The Summary* 1.10–11.
52. Nagao, *Shōdaijōron*, commentary to 2.33.

tent was respected as bedrock scriptural method in the West. That was considered crucial for an understanding of the text and what its inspired meaning might be.

In Yogācāra, one *must* take intent into consideration inasmuch as, through practice, one comes to share the Buddha's intent of compassionately liberating all beings. The Yogācāra philosophers in Buddhist India drew from their meditational practice—and from their analysis of mind—insights and interpretations they felt paralleled those of the Buddha author of their scriptures. They hardly ever filled in historical or contextual information, for this was not of interest to them. Only the intent of the Buddha toward awakening was of any import. We want to be awakened, not informed.

That awakening may be clarified both through conventional philosophy and through the meditative abandonment of all philosophy. In seeking to understand the intent in the words of scripture:

> [t]hrough a wisdom born from [hearing] the doctrine, the Bodhisattvas base themselves upon the words [of the scriptures], take the text literally and do not yet understand the intention . . . . Through a wisdom born from reflecting [on that doctrine], the Bodhisattvas do not base themselves upon the words or take the meaning literally and do understand the intention . . . . Through a wisdom born from meditation, the Bodhisattvas either base themselves on the words or do not, either take the text literally or do not, but, in understanding the intention, they see the heart of the matter through images understood in concentration.[53]

That is, the point is not to take the words of scripture themselves as containing meaning but, through the experience of concentration, to understand the meaning that those words were intended to express, to share the Buddha's intent. In other words, one is to duplicate the wisdom of the Buddha and become awakened. Only when one has to some extent understood this intention is it possible to do valid (as well as philologically researched) textual study.

A literalistic method of interpreting scripture is rejected, for that is yet another example of the imagined pattern of understanding. It would cling to words as if meaning were a property of speech rather than a function of understanding. But after having understood the intent of the scripture, one is then free either to stick close to the text or to recast it in

---

53. Keenan, *Scripture on the Explication*, 63–64.

other terms as appropriate. This is now possible because concentration has led one into the heart of the matter, into a personal and immediate understanding of the scripture—and the tradition—as empty of any speech or judgment and thus replete with the dependent arising of infallible and authentic teaching and doctrine. Those who cling to theological theory, or who adhere to a metaphysical refuge from change and pain, do not allow the soil of their minds to be receptive to the rain of Buddha teaching or gospel path and thus to become fertile soil for the implanted word. Their minds are rock hard and nothing ever grows there.

This hermeneutic—this method of interpreting scripture—is rooted in the practice of concentration. It focuses upon the understanding of religious meaning, both silent and enunciated, ultimate and conventional. It is not merely the result of logical reasoning or textual study. In Western scripture study, hermeneutic questions arise from considerations of literary analysis and have frequently been seen *in opposition* to religious practice. But in the monasteries of Buddhist India, textual interpretation flowed from understanding attained *through* the religious practice of meditation and concentration.

Middle Path philosopher Nāgārjuna, by emptying everything, had left the impression that no words mean anything. But the Yogācāra teachers, through their demonstration of the structure and functioning of mind, reclaimed a valid role for words in the realm of conventional truth. They maintained that the conversion of consciousness, which issues in perfected awakening, at the same time can reclaim as valid the other-dependent pattern of perceiving, thinking, and judging.

The other-dependent pattern of mind is the basic pattern, and it acts as a pivot. Most commonly, it swings toward the delusion of the imagined pattern but, upon conversion, it enables us to express meaning truthfully and validly. And so Yogācāra not only affirms ultimate meaning as the perfection of the Buddha's awakening, but it also commends worldly and conventional truth as the delusion-free teaching of an awakened mind. In the Yogācāra teachings of awakened wisdom, the truth of ultimate cessation and silence is twinned with worldly and conventional words, and silence reverberates into conventional speech rightly enunciated.

The Yogācārins make a distinction between false worldly convention and true worldly convention. The false mistakenly perceives essences in the images of things. By contrast, true worldly convention in an awakened person is grounded upon sound and valid perception of the senses, upon wise thinking, and upon that Buddha-mirror wisdom that reflects truth just as it is. An enlightened teacher inspects images, but without any assumption that an inner real self is grasping an outer real object. The awakened person knows that the object of scriptural interpretation is constructed meanings expressed through a revealed text—not the very nature of ultimate truth itself, which is always ineffable and silent. As mediated through words, doctrines are subject to intelligent and rational analysis. They are to flow stream-like through our lives and our cultures, but not to pool and become stagnant, or congeal into the icy dogma of a hardheaded and biased believer.

As the Middle Path philosophers taught, the truth of ultimate meaning transcends all reasoning. It is not a meaning brought about through any conscious operation. It is attained only in a quietude experienced as a non-attainment; it does not function through images; it is ineffable; it severs all expression; and it severs all disputation. The Yogācārins, too, insisted on the utter ineffability and transcendence of ultimate truth beyond all language. And yet, they raised conventional truth above commonsense errors and elevated it to language-formed doctrine and teachings. These conventional teachings occupy a humanly limited, but valid and efficacious, role in directing the flow of religious teachings. Indeed, scripture itself, as revealed into our languages, is conventional. What else could it be?

The Yogācārins argued that, once consciousness is converted from the imagined pattern, it can go on to engage in true and proper reasoning in the teaching of the scriptures and skillfully embody that teaching in ever new forms of doctrinal discourse.

4

Grounding Our Faith in a Pluralist World

Apologetics from the ground

A MAHĀYĀNA PHILOSOPHY, BY its very rejection of viewpoints, de-
motes the conclusions in all philosophy books. Consequently, in
wrapping up our recommendation to adopt, and adapt, the Mahāyāna
philosophies of Middle Path and Yogācāra in considering religious pluralism, we will remain within the purview of the world and of conventional
truth, eschewing any all-encompassing summation. These philosophies
will come alive, not in forming final conclusions, but only in the practice
of interfaith study and textual hermeneutic across cultures and traditions.
At least, that is the intent of this book—perhaps more modest than these
philosophies in their original Buddhist context, but potentially useful to
religious thinkers in a pluralist world.

The faith and practice of the religions are based on scripture and
molded by traditions rooted in the actual, vernacular lives of people. But
for sacred texts and teachers of the various religious traditions to serve
once again as creative and liberating forces in their respective cultures
today, they need an injection of freshly expressed, insightful theologies
and persuasive apologetics newly crafted to speak to a world of multiple
faiths.

The Mahāyāna patterns of thought introduced here would enable
each religious tradition to develop a clear apologetic discourse, not as
the last word to be uttered, but as a valid, true, indefectible, and beautiful
conventional expression of its faith and a guide to its path of practice.
Freed from the false necessity of developing an apologetic that encloses
truth within a single religion, each faith community can with confidence

root the practice of its faith in the inherited wisdom of its particular vernacular tradition.

As we rewrite our theologies and rearticulate our apologetics, Mahāyāna would urge us to keep our claims in line with our ability to receive revelation, bringing us to and nesting us within our cultural ground while recommending respect for the insights of revelations received by others. One can practice a religion only on the ground.[1] One does not practice it by denigrating other traditions. It is enough to have a path revealed by the Lord Jesus—or Allah through the prophet Muhammad, or the Buddha—and to follow that path, all the while respecting and cherishing brothers and sisters from other traditions, indeed cherishing those traditions themselves as far as we may be able. Exposure to different traditions will raise in us important questions and engender deep thinking and theological engagement. None of that is to be avoided—it is all gift.

People of faith live themselves into their scriptures, and our traditions guide us in how to read and live those sacred texts. Scriptures—Muslim, Jewish, Buddhist, Christian, Taoist, Hindu—indeed have the authority to guide and direct our lives, but their authority can be exercised only *within* a tradition. Not only we ourselves, but even our scriptures possess no lunar view, no perspective from above by which to judge between traditions. We human beings grow from the ground of our cultures and our faiths. With the guidance of our respective scriptures and teachers, we are to learn the mind of Christ, to be ever more truly the servants of Allah, to follow Torah faithfully, to gain knowledge of Brahman, to be awakened as a buddha. And we are to respect scripture, even if—as the Zen masters say in their shockingly contrary way—from time to time one needs its pages at toilet. That very unusual and disconcerting recommendation, after all, merely emphasizes the sacred role of scripture in the first place. But all traditions teach that in order to study those scriptures we need

---

1. Or as James Heisig describes it, slightly above the ground. See his *Dialogues At One Inch*, in particular the three essays directly treating dialogue: "Converting Buddhism to Christianity, Christianity to Buddhism," 105–120, "Interreligiosity and Conversion," 121–58, and "Six Sūtras on Dialogue," 139–58. Heisig argues that, besides the particular traditions, there has come to be in modern culture a spiritual common sense, not only that we must live together, but that truth is multiform and found everywhere throughout the faith traditions (129), that truth is universal not uniform (114), and so recommends both a grounding in one language and culture (132) and that sound common sense of multiform truth.

commentaries—the Jewish Talmud, the Christian Fathers, the Buddhist *śāstras*—and the guidance of good friends and advisors.

Culturally sensitive hermeneutics

Christians do possess a theological guide for understanding the word of God in scripture. During the first five centuries of our tradition, the Church Fathers adopted terms and ideas from Greek philosophy to delineate the doctrine that the word of God from the beginning was embodied in the quite human person of Jesus. They used those philosophical concepts in working out the confessional creeds—rather unique to the Christian faith—as *symbola fidei*, sacraments of faith understanding.[2] The Nicene and Apostles' Creeds, which we regularly recite as part of our liturgy, support and engender our faith, indeed our belief, but they do not and cannot capture or arrogantly delimit that faith. They never were meant to do so. We call them simply creeds, confessional commitments of faith—not explanations of theology.

Moreover, these creeds are certainly not statements of Christian metaphysics, although they do employ some metaphysical terms borrowed from the Greeks and reworked in the Christian context, such as *homoousios*, describing how Jesus is "of one being" with the Father. Nor are they once-and-for-all-time expositions, for they live and breathe the cultural and philosophical origins of our early Christian fathers and mothers. So we cherish them and make them our own, and they in turn engender further statements of faith. And that has been the actual development of Christian doctrine for two millennia now.

Especially is the unfinished nature of the Christian creeds to be stressed in this book, wherein we see Greek patterns of thought as but one—albeit once elegant and persuasive—reading of the gospel. The Greek thought pattern and its language are for the most part incomprehensible to our modern cultures. But this need not mean that we overturn all our traditions, surrender the faith of our ancestors, or grow somehow out of our faith and culture. It does mean that in order to reclaim the faith of past centuries, contemporary Christian thinkers need first to retreat from everyday life to some quiet corner in which to study and learn languages and patterns of thought now long forgotten—the theologies and creeds of our ancestors—for when one enters into and moves within those classical

---

2. See Pelikan, *Credo*, for the full treatment.

worlds, they shine with a splendor bright and cheery. But then Christian thinkers need to go beyond that cultural framework, for to insist that this ancient metaphysical theology is normative for all is to shackle the gospel to now archaic philosophies and force it to hobble about crippled in a world of quick thinkers and restless seekers.[3]

The word of God dwells in the scriptures. Islam confesses that the Holy Qur'an is not only the word of Allah as an outflow into human language, but plain and simply the uncreated word of Allah, and thus the final revelation and seal to all others. It is this confession that sets Islam apart as the exclusive truth among religions. For Hindus, scripture is the explication of deeper and unannounced experiences best guarded in the silence of cessation or union with Brahman. In Buddhism, revelation is ongoing; it is not fixed and never closed into a universally accepted canon.[4]

The inspiration of revealed scriptures does not signify that they are immune to every kind of error. The Christian norm for understanding scripture, in fact, is that the Word of God dwells therein as it dwells in the person of Christ. That is, the Word of God for us is, like Jesus, fully human and fully divine; it is fully a construct of culture and fully a revelation from God, and yet without mixing what it means to be human with what it means to be divine. The inspired text remains fully a text, with all the moves of a text, with all the imperfections of writing, with all the erroneous assumptions of its authors, and with all the cultural cross-referencing and deferral textual words always have to other texts and other words.

---

3. I think this is what James Arraj, *Crucible of East-West Dialogue*, actually does by insisting on Neo-Scholastic philosophy as the necessary cultural basis for Christian faith. In this he agrees with Pope Benedict that Christianity itself is a culture. I would disagree, for then Christian faith must drag in its train a single system of philosophy which, although elegantly concise and persuasively reasoned, has passed from the consciousness of moderns everywhere. The problem is not the persuasiveness or adequacy of Neo-Scholastic thinking, of Gilson or Maritain, but the simple historical passing of their thought from Christian awareness. One could indeed employ Gilson's *Being and Some Philosophers*, to derive a similar critique of Mahāyāna philosophy, for Gilson's refutation of attempts to think beyond being can be applied to Buddhist emptiness beyond being. Arraj's measure is clear and he uses it often to dismiss those who differ; but he is, in the last analysis, unaware of the many philosophies of the world and is forced to retreat from the multiple modern cultures and their many philosophies altogether.

4. Buddhists have on occasion tried to reconcile divergent teachings that appear in their scriptures, but just as often they sidestep such issues by appealing to other scriptures considered more central to Buddhist traditions.

Thus, although inspired, the text may not only err in some peripheral matters (geographical and historical details, for instance), but also apparently accept ancient customs that were normative in their day but are no longer so (slavery, the stoning of a woman caught in adultery), and even make inaccurate statements about more central concerns like the imminent end of the present world and the coming of the last days. In other words, our scriptures demonstrate all the contingencies of their time and place.[5]

Nor is scripture to be looked to as a record of historical facts. No one has ever thought it useful to try to reconstruct or recover the historical Buddha from the Buddhist scriptures. This is so, not only because the extant texts are so late (the earliest Mahāyāna scriptures did not appear until some five hundred years after the passing of the historical Buddha, and the Hīnayāna sources themselves are fully a few hundred or so years after the events), but also because the story of the Buddha is a paradigm, not an historical presentation. And history in Buddhism as in Hinduism, no matter how accurate, is seen not as enlightening, but as merely the sad account of human delusion, war, and suffering.

Indeed, until Herman Samuel Reimarus in the eighteenth century,[6] no one ever tried to write a life of Jesus. And reverence for scripture and tradition should not lead contemporary Christians to a wooden approach to a history that makes supernatural assertions and insists on a concocted history of Jesus and the first century. This might preserve tradition but only as an interesting episode in an imagined past. In an incarnational faith like the Christian one, history is *our* history, our history in English, in Chinese, in Russian, in Swahili. If we live as the body of Christ, we need no Jesus seminar to tell us all about Jesus, for he has sent his spirit (*rūah*) into our hearts that she might guide us to witness to him, to preach his gospel, and to dedicate our lives to his mission.

Reading scripture to learn how Jesus embodied himself not only in his body but also in his time, and how the Church took root and grew

---

5. Biblical literalists, however, would not accept this understanding of scripture. In the words of seventeenth-century Lutheran theologian J.A. Quenstedt: "[I]n canonical Sacred Scripture there is no lie, no falsehood, not even the tiniest of errors, either in content or in words. Rather, each and every thing contained in it is altogether true, be it dogmatic or moral or historical, chronological, topographical, or onomastic. It is neither possible nor permissible to attribute to the amanuenses of the Holy Spirit any ignorance, lack of thought, or forgetfulness, or any lapse of memory in recording Holy Writ." As quoted in Pelikan, *Christian Tradition* 4:343–44.

6. Pelikan, *Christian Tradition* 4:361–62.

throughout the ancient world, should lead us to do the same in our time. We should attempt to read creatively in light of *our* cultures, sinking our roots in the here and now, and in the gospel traditions. Scripture is revealed as the Word enfleshed in particular living languages and cultures, entirely human and entirely open to interpretation by later commentators and teachers and formed upon the experiences of later practitioners. Because so totally open, it is divinely inspired. As Gregory of Nyssa teaches, our stretching forth for God is an endless questing forth from glory to glory, from one enlightenment to the next, and I would add, from one commentary to another. When God speaks scripture, revealed speaking comes into being. But all words are incarnated as human.

Truth and convention

Because our insights about religion are grounded in time, space, and practice, they can never be more than virtually true. None of us are heirs to an absolute truth that would authorize us to use force in bringing others to assent to it; all crusades are abominations and deeply sinful. We are human, and we can never entertain or answer all the relevant questions about the deep things of the spirit. For Christians, for example, ever-new dimensions to our understanding of being one with Christ still await discovery.

In this spirit, we Christians need to pursue our religious practice humbly, without bloated claims to possessing a cultureless, universally uniform, and ungrounded truth, and without the extrusion of our claims into broad metaphysical systems. I believe that Aristotle was the first to use the word "metaphysics." He had just written a book called *Physics*, in which he treated the things of this sensed, empirical world. After completing this work, he wrote another about being as being, its form, matter, nature, etc. This book he called *Metaphysics*, meaning either simply that these topics came "after" (meta) physics, or that these themes were "higher than" and "above" (meta) our physical and empirically sensed world. It is in this latter meaning that the word metaphysics has come down to us. Christians have tended to regard metaphysics as a super-structure that is built upon the natural, organic, physical world that we experience, forming indeed the very structure of reality. But metaphysical superstructures, no matter how elegant, are rigid. Built upon the shifting sands of particular life circumstances and out of the swirl of the dependently arising world of our ongoing experience, they can never be true to the life circumstances of others, and over time become questionable refuges even for ourselves.

The Mahāyāna approach leaves in a quandary those who would cling to such rigid structures of theological theory or metaphysical truth, for they cannot open their minds to be changed by ever deeper contemplation of scriptural teachings and doctrine, even their own. Their refuge against change and pain is unquestioning adherence to literal and controllable affirmations and vociferous claims that attempt to draw people to their version of the faith by the volume of their voices and in the process give that faith a bad name. They construct gateway problems for themselves and others, because the entrance into doctrine they will not swing open for themselves, nor will they allow others to open that gate and enter into the doctrine. Jesus calls them hypocrites because their faith is but pretense for self-interested security. Buddha calls them *icchantika*, for they do not desire true awakening, instead preferring to cling for safety and comfort to their own cherished religious views.

Christians' experience of God in Christ does shift over time. Modern Christian practitioners experience oneness with Christ in ways that the ancient apostles and saints could not have imagined.[7] Indeed, we now understand that our cosmos may have no finite outer limit and thus—given the theology that Jesus Christ is the human and terrestrial incarnation of a God too immense to fathom and too elusive to stage-manage to our own benefit—this leaves open questions about the cosmic significance of Christ. We might wonder whether there are alien intelligences that are saved in other ways.[8] Perhaps surprisingly, a theology book I read in seminary several decades ago taught in an aside (scholion) that there might indeed be different incarnations of the Word to other beings in other worlds. Jesus is human, of this earth, one of us. But God is not limited to just this incarnation and the Martians might indeed, if ever there were any, have needed a different incarnation. The upshot of all this is

7. See Pelikan, *Jesus Through the Centuries*, on the weaving of culturally regnant images of Jesus within the Christian world. It matters immensely whether one sees Jesus as the Cosmic Logos or as the Liberator.

8. The theme of Russell's *Sparrow* and *Children of God* is that we earthlings discover such a place, and the first spaceship to go there is sent by Jesuits to bring them our gospel. Another possible story line would have Jesuit missionaries arriving and finding there a people who celebrate a different incarnation of the Word.

that judgments of truth—even religious truth—are at best, as Lonergan asserts, "virtually unconditioned," which is to say, always contextual and always vernacular.[9]

A philosophy of religions informed by the Mahāyāna way of thinking would not require any mapping of the territory of other religions, because awareness of the conventional nature of truth relieves us of the need for a map of reality. We do not need to pretend that we comprehend everything. There are no satellite pictures to gaze upon, and no diagram will offer the comforting assurance that we have it all right. No single picture, no big picture, and no picture gallery. No guarantees anywhere—just grounding in practice and faith thinking. Here, "truth" describes particular events whereby faith and doctrine lead people from language to silence, and then from silence back again to language, to enunciate doctrine and to engage in the world on its own terms. Truth, then, is not univocal—one in meaning for all persons—but context-dependent and variable.

A philosophical practice that employs Mahāyāna concepts would focus on concrete and skillful means, and on conventional truth and doctrine. It would avoid the "thin and skinny" approach of squeezing the traditions for their bottom-line truth claims, lining up one against the other and adjudicating their validity. In such skinny analyses we are left, not with the fibrous and rich fruits of our multiform humanness, but with uninteresting bottles of concentrated fruit juice, peach drink instead of those luscious peaches summer brings us Vermonters from the south. Even a thoroughly pluralist admission of the validity of all claims still functions in the thin and rarefied atmosphere of truth claims ripped from their historical contexts of practice and insight, and pressed into the terms of some assured higher knowledge or meta-language. In a Mahāyāna context, by contrast, one may study the traditions of others in the richness of their myriad insights and, in the realization that all faith must be grounded, learn of the experiences of faith and practice that undergird the truth claims affirmed in their doctrines.

If, for example, anyone wishes to understand the christological formulas of the early ecumenical councils, they need to become familiar with the thick texture of now-ancient Greek philosophies about person and nature. This is no easy task, for no one functions today with the Greek notion that an "essence" is much more real than any individual example

9. Lonergan, *Insight*, 728–35, and throughout the book.

of that essence. (In the Greek context, for example, "dog-ness" would be more real than my dog Duke.) Only if that old context is grasped and its argumentation learned and felt, can we understand that the confession that Jesus is divine is not a claim that this particular person among all persons is God. Rather it is an assertion that, because Jesus is the incarnate Word, humanity and God are united. In the incarnation of the divine word, we become "deified" by grace. Christological doctrine is not about Jesus or God "out there," but about us in our journey into oneness with God through Christ.

Likewise, the Buddhist doctrine of no-self, in its native soil, is not about a pessimistic view of human development. It is about shifting the center of identity from delusion to awakened wisdom. No-self does not function within the spectrum of Western ideas about personhood and soul, but rather hodologically—that is, path-oriented—as an antidote to what Jews, Christians, and Muslims would describe as arrogance and pride. One learns of the practice of no-self either personally and internally through meditation and struggle, or second-handedly through long and patient study of Buddhist traditions, which may in their turn lead us to meditation and struggle.

The richness of any faith tradition is found not in its denuded truth claims but rather enmeshed in the complicated webs of insight and meaning that reflect the practice of that faith and support its claims. If we brush aside those webs and ignore their source in the rich and living ecosystems from which they spring, we wind up with but the carcasses of desiccated truths.

With the notion of the two truths, the Mahāyāna philosophers guard against claims that this or that teaching is the culmination. Their insistence that only silence is ultimate serves, not as a ground upon which to validate claims, but as a guard against validating any claim as ultimate. One text says that the Buddha taught for forty years but never uttered a single world. Nāgārjuna negates his own cherished doctrine precisely because he cherishes that doctrine and does not want to fix it as some merely interesting laboratory specimen of a now past life. In this Mahāyāna light, religions—all sects of Buddhism and all other traditions—are deprived of their claimed ultimate status, simply but all-inclusively, because they are verbalized.

The fact that the doctrine of the two truths originates within the Mahāyāna Buddhist tradition need not deter others from considering its central precepts. It is expressed in various ways by such Western theologians as Abraham Joshua Heschel and in the presentation of apophatic and kataphatic theology in the letters of Dionysius.[10] And the fact that the doctrine of two truths constitutes a critique from within a central commitment to practice makes it all the more engaging. This was not conceived by disinterested academics who assume some objective, meta-religious stance but was developed from the exigencies of practice and aimed at a furtherance of such practice.[11] The two truths were developed in order to resolve a problem that all religious traditions have had to confront: how to communicate an ineffable experience.

The Emptiness and Dependent Arising of Traditions

The Mahāyāna concept of two truths—precisely because it empties all religious doctrine of absolute status—argues that we can indeed confess the truth of our own faith tradition while at the same time acknowledging that its truth is embedded within culture and historical circumstance. And the Mahāyāna understanding of emptiness and dependent arising—because it emphasizes ever more the web of historical causes and conditions—recommends deep and detailed study of both our own and others' religious traditions.

In this perspective, particular religious doctrines remain both true and particular. We may find analogues and parallels across traditions. Indeed, we would expect to so find such parallels. For example, the uniqueness of Christ in collapsing the boundaries between human and divine presents a Western and Greek understanding of the unity that is expressed in Mahāyāna as the identification of emptiness and dependent arising. The Christian insistence that the two natures of Christ are without confusion or commingling echoes the Mahāyāna disjunction between the two truths of ultimate meaning and worldly convention, for the ultimacy of emptiness transcends the conventional truth enunciated in the cultures of this world, while being at the same time identical with it.[12] Yet these

10. See Hathaway, *Hierarchy and the Definition of Order*, 154, who speaks of a symbolic theology of what is said, characterized as worldly, subject to custom, human, and mediated, and a negative theology of what is not said, characterized as aimed at purification, at non-defilement, beyond the world, and aimed at perfection. See Keenan, *Meaning of Christ*, 111–12.

11. See Keenan, "Emptiness as a Paradigm," 60.

12. For a Mahāyāna understanding of the Christian confession of Christ as human

doctrines remain particular to their traditions, and cross-cultural moves have to be made with care and concern for the integrity of faith.

The doctrines of any one religious tradition are not here brought into question, no matter how analogous the doctrines of different traditions may be. The focus of Mahāyāna philosophy is not on any particular apologetic or negation, but rather on understanding our human understanding of doctrinal affirmations and negations, and on validating our human traditions of faith just as long as they demonstrate their truth in their actions. That does not, however, mean that faithful people of any tradition cannot and do not sin, against others and against their own tradition. We do, and often. Crusades occur and holy wars abound. Catholics and Protestants are still wary of one another in Ireland. Muslims and Hindus have been known to riot and burn and kill. But these, no matter how horrendous their acts, represent but a comparatively small number of the faithful, even though their actions threaten war here or there, and thus everywhere for everyone.

Religious traditions are embedded within cultural experiences and histories that are not universally shared. Those experiences are modeled on the experiences of their founders, clearly different from one another, and over the ages they take on characteristic cultural features that guide and encourage—stained-glass images and statues together with pews, no-images and no-pews with rich rugs and beautiful prayer spaces. The quietude of Śākyamuni's awakening under the Bodhi tree contrasts mightily with the execution of Jesus in the cauldron of imperial Roman brutality in first-century Palestine. Religions come with their own distinctive flavors and textures. The finality of the revelation of the Qur'an to Muhammad, who attests to the God-given word in that he himself cannot even write, sweeps away all the varied distractions and plurality of the various gods, both in Western theologies and in the Arabian homeland. The traditions' founders and their ancestral homes are quite different, and their followers—according to the culture and time in which they live and practice—likewise differ.

Even when they dwell in the same land, the multiform experiences of faith practitioners in the many different religions are not entirely available to us. How could one possibly attend to all the relevant data about such varied experiences? In any case, the insights that flow from different

---

and divine, see Keenan, *Meaning of Christ*.

religious experiences are simply not attainable by taking a tour of inspection through the regions of other people's faith and practice. How is a Jew or a Muslim to attain insight into Hindu Vaiṣṇaivite or Śaivite devotion before a statue of the Lord Krishna or the Lord Śiva? That deity's image itself occludes sympathetic understanding for a Jew or a Muslim, both of whom name but the one God and abhor graven images. How can a Christian—long forgetful of the brutality of the Crusades and the vicious pogroms of Europe, and simply unaware of the constant insults Christians hurled at Muslims in the first centuries of Islam[13] (that they had "bad" teachers, that Muhammad misunderstood his epileptic seizures as revelatory states)—understand the visceral rejection of the cross by Jews and Muslims who well remember being caught in its crosshairs and superseded by its brute power?[14] Indeed, how can Jews today appreciate the depth of Christian devotion to the redemptive power of the cross that brings life out of death, when for them it has most often brought only death out of life? How could early Muslims appreciate the doctrines of Incarnation and Trinity, when they were innocent of the Greek philosophical idiom in which those doctrines are embedded? And when the only Christians they directly encountered were monophysites (those "bad" teachers), who seemed to claim simply that Jesus was of only one, divine, nature?

A Mahāyāna philosophy of religions can perhaps offer a rather content-neutral approach to people of the various faith traditions in their thinking about the multitude of religions in this world. It would recommend committed practice of one's own faith, grounded upon its dependently arisen history. It would call for patient and respectful dialogue with other traditions in all the rich "thickness" of their many experiences, insights, and doctrines. And it would encourage further meditation on the meaning of personal doctrines long held and not about to be abandoned.

The Middle Path and Yogācāra notions outlined above—of emptiness and dependent arising, of the two truths, and the patterns of consciousness—were employed by the Mahāyāna thinkers to deepen older Buddhist teachings about skillful means—in interpreting scripture and in teaching doctrine. We can learn from this tradition of regarding religious teaching as a skillful means to lead people toward awakening, to break

13. See Daniel, *Islam and the West*, and Hoyland, *Seeing Islam*. The first centuries of Christian responses to early Islam were ignorant dismissals and blithe caricatures.

14. Carroll, *Constantine's Sword*, 3–5, and throughout the book.

through their tenacious delusions and long-entrenched habits of clinging to images. These are the always-dangerous graven images, set up in
the mind of an already dead faith. In the Mahāyāna view, the "truth" of
a teaching is not a normative set of yes-or-no propositions but rather a
dexterous weaving of insight and judgment attuned to the needs of the
listener at a particular time and place. And yet it is indeed true and not
dispensable. It is related to time and culture but never merely relative, for
the traditions and their teachings lead to that silence wherefrom doctrine
and faith emerge. Maximus the Confessor has it that "the doctrines of the
Church are superseded by their own content."[15]

That which is truly unconditioned—whether in the theistic faiths
or in Buddhist wisdom—lies beyond and apart from all conditions of
human understanding and judging. Indeed, it has no conditions to be
fulfilled and no data that might be organized into intelligible patterns. For
Buddhists, this is the unconditioned state of the realm of the real, or cessation. For Muslims, it is Allah the Merciful. For Vedantists, it is knowledge
of "brahman without any characteristics";[16] and for Vaiṣṇavites, devout
oneness with Lord Krishna. For Christians, it is falling in love with God,
entering into the dark cloud of unknowing, being one with the ultimate
source of all intelligence and love. And faith is the knowledge that flows
from being in love with God. That dynamic state of love justifies itself just
as any dynamic state of falling in love, for it stands in need of no further
validation. Being in love validates itself.

Interfaith conversation in a Mahāyāna mode

Although a Mahāyāna philosophy of religions will challenge the immutable and normative certitude of all traditions and all viewpoints, it does
not merely reduce religious traditions to cultural constructs. It does not
preclude faith and certitude—it affirms them. Just as we are happily dependent for each breath on the creative act of God, so faith is celebrated
by acknowledging the dependence of one's own tradition on its history
and in recognizing that religious truth claims are all embedded within
a culture and a context. Faith must be grounded in the very concrete
and historical certainty that one's tradition does lead into the mystical
realm of silence, awe, and wonder, thence to reengage awakened minds

15. Cited in Pelikan, *Christian Tradition*, 2:30–31.

16. Sanskrit: *nirguṇa brahman*.

into everyday worlds where they may carry out the tasks of intelligence and compassion, seeking justice and working for peace. This is true religion—visiting the marginal and refusing to make rash judgments.[17]

To Christians, a Mahāyāna philosophy of religions can offer fresh patterns of thinking that will enable us to enunciate the gospel in strong and concrete ways that are vernacular and conventionally true.[18] (Only God is absolute, and in the New Testament God speaks hardly at all. As Ignatius of Antioch remarked, Jesus is the speaking of God from silence to us.) Further, Mahāyāna can help us to understand other religions as fraternal faith traditions that are valuable in themselves and valuable to us because of their teachings. They are valuable in themselves because of the many millions of people they bring to spiritual maturity, an obvious fact to anyone who lives among Buddhists, Muslims, Jews, or Hindus. They are also valuable to us, for in dialogue they have the power to trigger insights into our own most cherished and fundamental doctrines.

It is most helpful, for example, to hear a Jewish or Muslim sister question the notion of the Incarnation and assert how irrational it seems. They are on target: our Christian claim beggars the imagination and demands a full and deep rethinking both of what it means to be human, for God becomes human, and what it means to be God, for God becomes human. Surely, in the doctrine of Incarnation the notion of God, beyond time and space, unchanging and immutable, is shaken to its philosophical foundation.[19] Indeed, the medieval theologians knew this well, for they intentionally avoid talking of God changing or becoming. They speak only of God "moving" to become human, or of God's actions "*ad extra*" (externally) and "*quoad nos*" (as they appear to us), not of God's actions "*ad intra*" (internally) or "*quoad se*" (as they are in themselves). These are

17. See Keenan, *Wisdom of James*, 36–41, 60–63, and 78–81.

18. See Heisig, *Dialogues At One Inch*, 113.

19. With this incarnational faith as our base belief, it would indeed be salutary for Christians to engage Jews and Muslims in conversation on the doctrines of Incarnation and Trinity. They have been critiquing these doctrines for centuries and have seldom ever received a thoughtful response—except perhaps for the abandonment of these very doctrines by embarrassed Christians who themselves have failed to attend to these teachings. Historically, Christians have responded to Muslims by simply ignoring and insulting them, dismissing their claims. Even when Aquinas wrote his *Summa Contra Gentiles*, the "gentiles" in his account—oddly enough—were the Jews and the Muslims. Neither Aquinas nor his contemporaries, however, thought it necessary actually to talk doctrine with Jews and Muslims.

simply rhetorical moves, but they signify that we Christians are aware of a host of problems if God can become anything God was not, for that limits God to time and space.[20]

On the other hand, it is eye opening to hear a Hindu tell us that incarnations are no problem, for in theistic Vaiṣṇaivism and Śaivism there are many incarnations, and God is always taking on a form tailored to the needs of beings at that moment. A Buddhist in this discussion might proffer the notion of the "transformation body" of a Buddha. Christians would not accept such incarnations[21] or transformation bodies,[22] for invariably these are understood in a docetic manner, as God taking on an external appearance only. Still, such a discussion can be most helpful to Christians today precisely because most have little notion of what their own doctrine of Incarnation does in fact affirm. Without deeper thought on the issue, many seem to think that Jesus is a supernatural being come to birth on Christmas and to rise on Easter.

We live among the many religious traditions and many faiths and many philosophies. Open-minded people recognize stellar persons such as Socrates and Nietzsche among the philosophers, with Christians they cherish Jesus, with Mormons they admire the faith and bravery of Joseph Smith, and with Baha'is they appreciate Bahā 'Allah (Mīrzā Husayn 'Alī Nūri)—for all of the words of all foundational thinkers and preachers are regarded by some as canonical. (Nietzsche stands as the most anti-canon canonical thinker at the beginning of modern critical culture.) The options are many; but still, for the most part and usually, we belong to one tradition or another. There are a few dual citizens who affirm two traditions, but to date they remain something of an exception.[23] Mahāyāna can

---

20. Here one might consult Charles Hartshorne and John Cobb on process theology of God as the emergent élan of the universe. Cobb once remarked in private conversation that he spent years in the Cobb-Abe dialogues on Christianity and Buddhism trying to explain to Zen philosopher Masao Abe that God signifies "the prime instance of dependent arising," but Abe never got the point. Indeed for a Buddhist, dependent arising deals with the samsaric world of suffering—or in its Mahāyāna version, the conventional world of suffering and cessation—but never the ultimate, which is indicated by the silence of the Dharma realm or some such synonym.

21. Sanskrit: *avatāra*.

22. Sanskrit: *nirmāṇa-kāya*.

23. See the essays in Cornille, *Many Mansions?* Also Rose Drew, "An Exploration of Buddhist Christian Dual Belonging," Ph.D. thesis, University of Glasgow, Scotland, 2008.

aid in opening us all to truth wherever it may be found, for Mahāyāna affirms our traditions both as ours and as true.

Encounters among world religions today are still moved for the most part by an agenda of histories to be avoided: crusades, jihads, pogroms, the Shoah, the beheadings and burnings of "heretics" in European ecclesiastical and dynastic struggles, wars against perceived evildoers. And for want of rich and detailed understanding of the languages and traditions of one another, the frameworks of discussion, at their best, tend toward prescriptive ideas about how religions "should" relate. At their worst, we line up religions into competing systems and manage somehow always to denude other faiths of their rich and beautiful adornments and life, expose the now unrobed nakedness of their failures and misconceptions, and reject them as either surely false or certainly lesser.

The first step toward resolving such an impasse is to empty all our preconceptions, reject all picture frames, methods, and programs, and listen to one another in depth and detail. No exclusivist sectarian affirmations. No graded, inclusivist notions that other people have pieces of my full truth. And no vapid affirmations that all religions are, each and every one, paths up the same mountain, equally valid approaches to an unnamable absolute—or indeed that each leads to a different mountain and a different summit.

For all of these theories, I would substitute an approach based on Mahāyāna emptiness, and in practice I would follow the pattern of comparative study exemplified primarily by the works of Francis X. Clooney, James L. Fredericks, and Joseph S. O'Leary. Their inclusivist approaches are non-graded, accepting this world of many faiths as it is given in our histories. Their approach recommends itself as a way of open-mindedly accepting other traditions from within the ground of one's own tradition. Comparative theologians Clooney and Fredericks, for example, insist upon careful, patient reading and contextual understanding of other traditions, eschewing caricatured depictions of the other.[24] These two Christian thinkers contend that comparative theology and interfaith study must be done in depth and detail, and that one cannot move swiftly and blithely to draw conclusions about other traditions, for first and importantly one has to attend broadly to the culture and the teachings of the other and then

---

24. See especially Clooney on comparative theology, *Theology After Vedānta*, 4–13; Fredericks, *Faith among Faiths*, 139–61; and Fredericks' *Buddhists and Christians*, where he interweaves Buddhist and Christian themes within his comparative theology.

work to understand the import and impact of doctrine within its context. Only then can one begin to adjudicate issues of truth and to bring the doctrines of others into dialogue with one's own tradition.

In a word, Clooney and Fredericks counsel patience and engagement. Their approaches affirm that other traditions, despite the mutations one can indeed find in each, entice not toward error, but stretch forth toward insight and practice perhaps unknown to us. O'Leary treats religions as conventions and delves into the past of our Christian history and of Buddhist philosophy with a skill learned over the last number of decades living and teaching in Japan.[25] Such comparativist thinkers confess that they themselves become enriched and formed by what they study and read so carefully, so that when they return to the texts of their own tradition, they read with new eyes and refreshed minds.[26] It is with such an enriched mindset that they embrace and thus include the faith of others, and that faith becomes part of their understanding of the Christian gospel. Thus, they insist that there is a vital need to explore other religions, and to dialogue with their followers, without abandoning one's own faith and without prejudging that the viewpoints of one's native faith will win out in the end. This non-graded inclusivism remains faithful to our own faith while deepening our understanding of others.

I would seek to further these open-minded and open-ended interfaith efforts by offering the riches of Mahāyāna thought as a philosophical basis for their endeavors. Although Mahāyāna Buddhism as a religious tradition is specifically enculturated within Indian, Chinese, and Japanese Buddhist cultural discourse and it does embrace specific practices of concentration and meditation, it need not privilege one religious tradition over another. Indeed, it can aid us in crafting an informed apologetics for Christianity, for Islam, for each faith tradition—apologetics that do not commit the common errors of simply misunderstanding or being unaware of the impact of history on our discourse. Apologists will have to buy new dictionaries: Farsi, Sanskrit, Arabic, Greek, and so forth. And, apologists will have to study the doctrinal histories of others, for without that work, the usual misinterpretations will ensue: that Buddhism is pessimistic, that Christianity is supernatural fancy, that Islam is warlike—all canards and

25. See O'Leary, "Religions as Conventions," especially the section "De-absolutizing Religion," 415–19, and his "Emptiness and Dogma," 227–45.

26. Clooney, "Reading the World in Christ," 66–72. See also Knitter, *Theologies of Religions*, 202–15.

caricatures with some basis on experienced reality. A Mahāyāna approach will empty any religious truth of any final validity, only to reaffirm the traditions in their historical and dependently arisen specificity.

For a theologian in today's world, dialogue is not an optional activity, as if theology could still function within its accustomed classical culture with its conceit of universally valid theological norms. Monocultural, blinkered theology does more to drive people from churches and temples than any scandal or sin ever did. We are all well able to recognize and forgive human brokenness and frailty; we want it stopped, immediately, but we do understand. The real obstacle to participation in faith communities today is rather arrogance and pride, even when clothed in claims of revealed and assured truth. We can well enough practice our faith with commitment and still engage one another at the deepest of human levels, studying one another's texts and traditions deeply and with respect, and engaging in ongoing dialogue. Dialogue flows directly from our human awareness of our contingent histories and traditions.

Dialogue with other religious traditions is regarded by some, however, with great trepidation. And indeed, new insight into the beauty and the efficacy of other traditions can be unsettling. Some will draw back from a close encounter with an unfamiliar tradition and the dislocation it might entail, slipping into the easy distancing that renders all faith innocuous and life insipid. Others will be drawn to learn more of a "foreign" tradition, often—though not always—with the unanticipated result that they turn back to learn more deeply of their own tradition of origin.[27] Perhaps those who were never exposed to any deep inquiry into their own faith, who grew up in families whose practice was lukewarm, are more likely to seek out a new tradition. "Dangers" do abound. But by that very fact, we are impelled toward dialogue. The enemy of true faith, in all the traditions, is shallow complacency or gluey cultural adhesion, not knowledge of others.

The most fruitful dialogue has no rules of engagement or necessary stages—it is not a programmed activity.[28] Rather, it is open to the concerns

---

27. See Kasimow, Keenan, and Keenan, *Beside Still Waters,* for essays by fourteen Jews and Christians whose encounters with Buddhism strengthened and affirmed their inherited faith.

28. See van Bragt, "Shoshūkyō taiwa no shomondai" [Problems in Interreligious Dialogue], 45, who describes the aim of dialogue as aimless and without agenda. Rather, it is a "holy adventure" of people coming together to examine their common concerns

of the participants, whoever they may be and whatever their interests. I would argue that interfaith dialogue should be detailed and apologetic, with participants offering plausible defenses of and recommendations for their own native or chosen traditions. Those kinds of discussions have always been for me the most stimulating. I want to argue with cherished friends.

Participants in dialogue are in most cases persons who are deeply engaged in their traditions, although at times they are but superficial observers of the doctrines of other people. A dialogue between engaged practitioners who are richly familiar with one another's ideas and practices can be grounded upon an increasingly shared history of interfaith events and may offer robust but sensitive apologetic defense of traditions inherited or adopted, without repeating the polemics (*polemos* = warfare) of the past. For this kind of dialogue, then—no rules, just conferences! We have of late become caught up in a panoramic mapping of theologies of religion that serves only to convince people that all religions are equally meaningless. Distrust the maps. Come to ground on the good earth somewhere, and let's talk.[29]

Wrapping up (a non-conclusion)

Mahāyāna—with its insistence that emptiness is the expeller of all views—can provide assistance in constructing new, dependently arisen models of understanding the doctrines of the traditions. A Mahāyāna approach to religious traditions is a practice of emptying our identities, with the deep hope that thereby we may regain those traditions and those identities, no longer as self-enclosed bastions of surety, but as historically conditioned and passionate embodiments of the traditions that guide us to truth and salvation. Such a focus on the traditions entails in fact a demotion of any overarching theology of religions, for no philosophy can pretend to map the rich experience of practitioners or to sketch what their insights are "really" about.

With the same historical focus, a Mahāyāna approach will make it crystal clear that the doctrines of the religions differ immensely, and that their repeated reclamation by practitioners signals the dependently arisen status of their language-formed conventional truth claims. In the present endeavor, Mahāyāna thought is meant to lead one to a heightened philo-

about one another, and about themselves.

29. Smith, *Map is Not Territory*, 289–309.

sophic awareness of the function and value of doctrine, both within one's native or chosen tradition, and in the traditions of other people. Should they adopt it, the practitioners of each tradition would be directed by this Mahāyāna approach both to meditate upon their culturally expressed and historical doctrine as a guide for practice, and to delve into the doctrines of others, all the while realizing that languages and cultures are conventional. Then and only then they are free to develop particular apologetics, not for all religious traditions, but for their own confessed tradition.

While a Mahāyāna philosophy of religions does challenge the normative certitude of all traditions and all viewpoints, it calls for faith to be grounded in the ability of each tradition infallibly and indefectibly to lead practitioners into silence, wonder, and awe, then to be brought back into more culturally identifiable realms in order to confess the creeds and embark on the practices that carry out the tasks of intelligence and compassion. Religious traditions may be said to be of "absolute" significance because of their historical salvific teachings and practices. And faith must be lived—again in Rahner's words—in "absolute affirmation." But this personal affirmation need not be validated by an appeal to metaphysical truth, symbolic reality, or universal principle. Rather, an absolute life-affirmation is validated through its ability to transform the individual within a particular cultural milieu, and the cultural milieu within that individual.

In both Christian and Buddhist traditions, an important aspect of this transformation is from selfishness to selflessness. In Islam, one converts from sin to obedience. Culturally presented affirmations of religious truth open doors for a variety of conventional paths without compromising the certainty that each individual receives from following a particular path. Mahāyāna thinking liberates religious traditions from the need to affirm metaphysical absolutes in order to be meaningful and valid. It liberates culture from the narrow-mindedness of a fear of missionaries. It liberates minds to rethink and delve deeper into their own faith traditions and to witness to the truth of those traditions. To fear a missionary from another tradition is already to admit that one's own tradition is incapable of engaging in robust dialogue and apologetics. From the Mahāyāna Buddhist perspective, since identifiable absolutes do not exist, we may indeed talk with one another, drink with one another, preach to one another, and steal elements from one another's tradition.[30]

We still do need clear apologetic expositions. All religions are driven to preach and to teach—to use words—and so doctrinal issues remain. Embarrassed or not, Buddhists still make claims. Ruefully aware though they are of the sad histories of some missions, Christians are still called to proclaim their gospel. As are Muslims, Hindus, and Jews. And their respective claims are not simply variations on the same theme. They are not all saying the same thing. Jesus the Christ figures centrally only in Christian discourse, although Muslims do recognize Jesus as a prophet and Buddhists as an enlightened master. Śiva is praised only in Vaiṣṇava theology. Apologetic issues do arise for Buddhists as well, for although all viewpoints are emptied of essential definition, they do not simply slither away down that slippery slope of relativism. That they do not do so becomes clear when we understand truth and truths in the context of the two truths—ultimate and conventional.

The philosophy of emptiness is not intended to present a static image of the truth of any reality. It is not a map of ultimate truth. Nor is it a sketch of conventional truth. It is not a map at all and sketches no overview of anything. That absence of a sketch will upset many people who, having like Moses caught a glimpse of God's backside, think they have grabbed him by the ass and are holding on for dear life. But God's backside is never grasped and I do not know just what Moses saw from the cleft of that rock.

The identity of emptiness and dependent arising, as well as the total disjunction between the truths of ultimate meaning and worldly convention are principles for living within the tensive dynamism of the path, a healthy "stretching forth" from everyday affairs to silent wonder, a straining to see in the dark, and a reinvigorated turning back from that wonder into our everyday worlds to reach out to all men and women.[31] Like the Buddha, we can experience silent awareness, but then we are returned to this world to work out the salvation of all beings in the creative interplay of skillful words and deeds, all the while aware that they never capture any ultimate.

30. See, for example, the textual borrowings discussed by Thomas, *Life of Buddha*, 237–48.

31. Keenan, *Meaning of Christ*, 93–103.

Emptiness and dependent arising take two approaches to the issues of being, winding up as two phases of the same insight. Together these two themes of the Middle Path—along with their elaboration in the Yogācāra understanding of consciousness—weave through our minds and bodies as guides along a moving path of wisdom and compassion. They, as we, are meant to be always on the move. All is transient, even philosophy. So, just as Nāgārjuna emptied his Buddhist tradition of its central teachings so as to reclaim that tradition in an engaged and grounded practice, Christians and Jews may at times also read their scriptures with an eye to the cultural constructs through which revelation comes, as would Hindus with their many scriptures, and Muslims with the Qur'an. Nothing is to be blithely discarded; everything understood and reclaimed. And we are to live on the move, in the truth of authentic prayer and practice.

Critical studies of religious history continually unearth insights long buried under cultural assumptions that prevailed earlier during the supposed unending and monolinear flow from a tradition's archetypal forebears down to its present-day practitioners.[32] And those assumptions change. American Catholics are not Irish Catholics. Indeed, Irish Catholics are not Irish Catholics anymore. As we come to understand ever more of our varied human histories, we are forced not only to rethink the past, but also to re-imagine our understanding of the gospel in the light of these new insights. And, although we may not read Western enlightenment writers much these days, their thought has permeated our culture and become its common sense: We demand reasoned approaches and are loathe to accept fanciful and magical ideas.

So today philosophies of religions are tricky. They move between the Scylla of narrow-minded religious belief, as sure of its truth as it is of the errors of all others, and the Charybdis of relativism, wherein all claims equally lose their moorings to any firm and stable basis. When Arnold Toynbee predicted that the major challenge to Christianity in the twentieth century would come not from Communism but from Buddhism, he was most perceptive. And Pope John Paul II echoed his evaluation.[33]

---

32. Perhaps Said's *Orientalism* is the classic study of the configurations through which one culture deals with and constructs another. Also see Karsh, *Islamic Imperialism*, for an account of Islam, not as the constant victim, but as itself culturally and politically powerful and indeed imperial.

33. See his letter "Dominus Jesus." For Toynbee see Dumoulin, *Christianity Meets Buddhism*, 31: "Arnold Toynbee once concluded a lecture with the remark that a future

Buddhism, at least in its Mahāyāna incarnation, challenges the normative certitude of all traditions, religious or philosophical. Mahāyāna insists on the humanness of our endeavors, even our faith endeavors. Often religions regard their revelations as transcendent to any cultural constructs, beyond all relativism. Many religious practitioners would feel uncomfortable to recognize the cultural relativity of their traditions. Many feel ill at ease with negating all other traditions. Most simply avoid the issue. Some people refuse to practice any religion because they find it unacceptable to think in the terms of any philosophy of religions. Often, regarding themselves as somehow beyond the traditions and thus innocent of lamentable religious histories, they cling to some amorphous individual or communal spirituality, imagining themselves to be somehow free when they are merely bereft. But there is no refuge in bereft or lonely experiences.

A philosophy of religions needs to account for the existence of the varying truth claims that are found among the world's diverse religious traditions. It needs to offer orientation to other peoples' religions—that we may indeed be open to them, yet without the need to abandon our own faith or collapse all faiths into mushy slurry. If we use the two truths as a model of religious experience, then we need not rush to adjudicate claims in interfaith dialogue by speedy appeal to the principle of logical consistency. Aristotle's logical law of contradiction states that of two propositions—one of which affirms something and the other of which denies the same thing—one is true and the other is false, if the sense of their affirmations is the same in both cases. That may indeed turn out to be the case—but if we are aware of the divergences of human experience and insight, we should approach the differences more gently and demand of ourselves a greater familiarity with the cultures and contexts from which claims draw their valence. Differences need not be exclusionary. They can be culturally perspectival.

Each tradition uses its own distinct set of basic terms so that—precisely because people are not actually speaking in the same context or about the same affirmation—often seemingly direct contradictions are not indicated, but variations of perspective drawn from sundry insights and discrete experiences.[34] Using the two truths as a model of religious

---

historian, writing a thousand years hence about the twentieth century, might take a greater interest in the first penetration of Christianity and Buddhism than in the disagreements between democratic and communist ideologies."

34. Lonergan, *Insight*, 734–35, about a plurality of metaphysics. I agree with the epis-

experience would provide a paradigm for religious pluralism that allows for different dependently arisen expressions of truth to co-exist without being ripped out of their individual contexts and drawn into direct confrontation with one another. We do not want to blend everything into one single taste, some religious cranapple juice.

Equally important, with its insistence on the validity of conventional truth and its acquisition, Mahāyāna also refuses to affirm that simply anything can be true. The tasks of a general apologetics for faith traditions remain urgent, but apologetics for particular traditions become more difficult, for nowadays one has to delve both into the faith traditions (one's own and another's) one wishes to compare and into the cultures in which they may be embodied. It is not enough to teach that, while Buddhists may believe in enlightenment, Christians place their faith in resurrection, when in our New Testament we have a text from Ephesians (4:14) that says, "Awake from your sleep, rise from the dead, and Christ will enlighten you." Our approach should be validated by its openness to others and perhaps by frank recognition of the ability of other traditions to accomplish their salvific purpose within their own dependently arisen frameworks.[35] Each tradition uses its own set of conventional truths in order to enable the practitioner to achieve a self-transformation. Such a recognition should at least be an operative assumption, because, as Bernanos and Rahner state so convincingly, God's grace is everywhere already,[36] and because all traditions aim to express verbal and conventional truths.

Using the two truths as a model for religious experience redirects interfaith dialogue away from a comparison of each tradition's notion of ultimate meaning to an analysis of each tradition's dependently arisen ideas and structures. The silence of ultimate meaning is by no means particular to Mahāyāna Buddhism. The ineffability of the central experiences of the traditions is perhaps the most universally shared theme in the scriptures

---

temology of Lonergan's *Insight*, but perhaps stress more than he did the cultural and linguistic differences of faith experiences and doctrinal insight. The traditions differ often in cultural terms and perspective, not diametrically, so that studies, such as Schmidt-Leukel's on creation by God or by karma can indeed bridge apparent contradictions by carefully attending to what is said in context.

35. The thesis of Heim, *Salvations*, as well as Kaplan's *Different Paths, Different Summits*.

36. Rahner, *Nature and Grace*, 35. Compare the ending of George Bernanos' *Diary of a Country Priest*—grace is everywhere, which seems to me to be a dramatic rendering of Rahner's point.

and commentaries of all traditions.[37] Anything beyond silence does injustice to the realization, for in the phrase of Gregory of Nyssa, when people talk about God, all are liars.[38] Yet a silence adhered to without exception imprisons any realization of ultimate truth within the mind of a single individual. If the realization cannot be expressed, then how can anyone else be led to attain it?

Different means of expression are necessary in order for the gospel to be meaningful to different people in different cultural contexts. "Hence to preach the gospel to all men calls for at least as many men as there are places and times, and it requires each of them to get to know the people to whom he is sent, their manners and styles and ways of thought and speech. There follows a manifold pluralism. It is primarily a pluralism of communication."[39] The teachings of the gospel or the Buddhist sūtras or the Qur'an must be communicated in a variety of different ways so that they can have meaning. Scripture "points to" ultimate meaning by making use of dependently arisen means of human expression. If it did not make use of such means, it could never point anywhere.

Since all religious traditions use dependently arisen myths, rituals, and doctrines to lead one toward an ultimate meaning that they themselves admit is beyond language, the two truths can be an engaging paradigm for understanding how mystic awareness is given expression in the world of mediated meaning and verbal articulation. Moreover, an understanding of all religious doctrine, myth, and ritual—indeed even of metaphysics as conventional truth—would facilitate dialogue between traditions, and free us from slavishly imitating the past. It would allow for faith and certainty without the need for universally normative proclamations and absolute truth-claims. It would help refocus such dialogue away from a simplistic comparison of the claims made by different traditions to an exploration of how the elements of each tradition are products of—and participants in—an authentic and indeed inspired dependently arisen culture and history; or how and why they are not. It would explore how each tradition's set of conventional truths represents a "means" towards self-transformation within certain horizons of meaning; and how they have been and can be distorted and deluded.

37. Keenan, "Emptiness as a Paradigm," 60.

38. Gregory of Nyssa, "On Virginity," *Patrologia Graeca*, 46:361a–b. For discussion, see Daniélou, *Platonisme et théologie mystique*, 265; also Keenan, *Meaning of Christ*, 98.

39. Lonergan, *Doctrinal Pluralism*, 23.

Emptiness is a vehicle for self-transformation, not a definitive picture of reality. Christians can be certain of Christ's transformative power without needing to insist that he be the one and only savior for those who have grievously suffered under the colonial power signed by his cross. We have failed Christ in those places, and our further insistence but drives the nails deeper. Still, Christians must indeed preach Christ to Muslims and Hindus, just as Muslims and Hindus must and may preach Islam and Viṣṇu. No one need pretend to an overarching vantage point under which all others can be subsumed. Christians can be comforted in knowing that their church helps them to lead a human life in prayer and commitment to others.

Dialogue *should not* be a threatening endeavor, for the transcendent truth of a given path has never been totally beyond cultural insight and judgment. Dialogue *should* be a threatening endeavor, for it will challenge our constructed sense of who we are and who we will be. Such a practice of dialogue does not suggest that one has the final truth, the globalizing truth, or all truths. Rather, it does suggest that we humbly follow vernacular traditions, as authentic and efficacious commitments of faith, in full entrustment to such traditions as worth dying for, but never as worth killing for. Such a radically humble commitment leaves one just as radically open to dialoging with and learning from other traditions. To do that, ratchet down the rhetoric and affirm the doctrines.

Bibliography

Allen, John L. *Pope Benedict XVI: A Biography of Joseph Ratzinger.* New York: Continuum, 2000.

Arraj, James. *Christianity in the Crucible of East-West Dialogue.* Midland: Inner Growth Books and Videos, 2001.

Asaṅga. *The Summary of the Great Vehicle (Mahāyānasaṃgraha).* Translated by John P. Keenan. Berkeley: Numata Center for Buddhist Translation and Research, 1992, 2003.

Bandhuprabha. *The Interpretation of the Buddha Land (Buddhabhūmyadeśa).* Translated by John P. Keenan. Berkeley: Numata Center for Buddhist Translation and Research, 2002.

Berger, Peter L. *The Sacred Canopy.* New York: Anchor Books, 1990.

Bernanos, George. *The Diary of a Country Priest.* New York: Image Books, Doubleday, 1960; first English printing 1928.

Berthrong, John H. *The Divine Deli: Religious Identity in the North American Cultural Mosaic.* Maryknoll: Orbis, 1999.

Bloom, Harold. *Jesus and Yahweh: The Names Divine.* New York: Riverhead Books, 2005.

Bonhoeffer, Dietrich. *Letters and Papers from Prison.* New York: Touchstone, 1997; first published 1953.

Cabezón, José Ignacio. *Buddhism and Language: A Study of Indo-Tibetan Scholasticism.* Albany: State University of New York Press, 1994.

Candrakīrti. *Lucid Exposition of the Middle Way: The Essential Chapters from the Prasannapada of Candrakīrti.* Translated by Mervyn Sprung. Boulder: Prajna Press, 1979.

Carroll, James. *Constantine's Sword: The Church and the Jews.* Boston: Houghton Mifflin, 2001.

Chatterjee, A.K. *The Yogācāra Idealism.* 2nd ed. Delhi: Motilal Banarsidass, 1972.

Chödrön, Pema. *When Things Fall Apart: Heart Advice for Difficult Times.* Boston: Shambala, 2000.

Clooney, Francis X. *Divine Mother, Blessed Mother: Hindu Goddesses and the Virgin Mary.* Oxford: Oxford University Press, 2005.

———. "Reading the World in Christ." In *Christian Uniqueness Reconsidered: The Myth of a Pluralist Theology of Religions,* edited by Gavin D'Costa, 61–80. Maryknoll: Orbis, 1990.

———. *Seeing Through Texts: Doing Theology among the Śrīvaiṣṇavas of South India.* Albany: State University of New York Press, 1986.

———. *Theology After Vedānta: An Experiment in Comparative Theology.* Albany: State University New York Press, 1993.

———. "When Religions Become Context." *Theology Today* 47.1 (1990): 30–38.

Bibliography

Cornille, Catherine. *Many Mansions? Multiple Religious Belonging and Christian Identity.* Maryknoll: Orbis Books, 2002.

Crowe, Frederick E. *The Lonergan Enterprise.* Boston: Cowley, 1980.

Dalai Lama. *Beyond Dogma: Dialogues and Discourses.* Berkeley: North Atlantic Books, 1996.

Daniel, Norman. *Islam and the West: The Making of an Image.* Oxford: One World, 1960, 2000.

Daniélou, Jean. *Platonisme et théologie mystique: Doctrine spirituelle de Saint Gregorie de Nysse.* Paris: Aubier, Éditions Montaigne, 1944.

Davies, W.D., and D.C. Allison, eds. *A Critical and Exegetical Commentary on the Gospel According to Saint Matthew.* 3 vols. London and New York: T&T Clark, 1991.

Dodd, C.H. *The Interpretation of the Fourth Gospel.* Cambridge: Cambridge University Press, 1953.

Dōgen. "Actualizing the Fundamental Point." In *Moon in a Dewdrop: Writings of Zen Master Dōgen.* Translated and edited by Kazuaki Tanahashi. San Francisco: North Point Press, 1985.

Dreyfus, George B.J. *Recognizing Reality: Dharmakīrti's Philosophy and its Tibetan Interpretations.* Albany: State University of New York Press, 1997.

Dumoulin, Heinrich. *Christianity Meets Buddhism.* Translated by John C. Maraldo. LaSalle: Open Court, 1974.

Dunne, John D. *Foundations of Dharmakīrti's Philosophy.* Boston: Wisdom Publications, 2004.

Dupuis, Jacques. *Toward a Christian Theology of Religious Pluralism.* Maryknoll: Orbis Books, 1997.

Eck, Diana L. *Encountering God: A Spiritual Journey from Bozeman to Banaras.* Boston: Beacon Press, 1993.

———. *A New Religious America: How a "Christian Country" Has Become the World's Most Religiously Diverse Nation.* San Francisco: Harper Collins, 2001.

Eliade, Mircea. *The Sacred and the Profane.* New York: Harcourt Brace and Co., 1954.

Faure, Bernard. *The Rhetoric of Immediacy: A Cultural Critique of Chan/Zen Buddhism.* Princeton: Princeton University Press, 1991.

Forman, Robert K.C. *Mysticism, Mind, Consciousness.* Albany: State University of New York Press, 1999.

Fredericks, James L. *Buddhists and Christians: Through Comparative Theology to Solidarity.* Maryknoll: Orbis Books, 2004.

———. *Faith among Faiths: Christian Theology and Non-Christian Religions.* Mahwah: Paulist Press, 1999.

Garfield, Jay L. *Empty Words: Buddhist Philosophy and Cross-Cultural Interpretation.* Oxford: Oxford University Press, 2002.

———. *The Fundamental Wisdom of the Middle Way: Nāgārjuna's Mūlamadhyamakakārikā.* Oxford: Oxford University Press, 1995.

Gilson, Étienne. *Being and Some Philosophers.* Toronto: Pontifical Institute of Medieval Studies, 1952.

Gregory of Nyssa. "On Virginity." In *Patrologia Graeca*, edited by J.P. Minge, 46:361a–b. Paris, 1857–66.

Griffiths, Paul J. *Problems of Religious Diversity.* Malden: Blackwell, 2001.

———. "Why We Need Interreligious Polemics." *First Things* 44 (1994): 31–37.

Haight, Roger. *Jesus: Symbol of God.* Maryknoll: Orbis Books, 1999.

Bibliography

Hakamaya, Noriaki. *Hihan bukkyō* [Critical Buddhism]. Tokyo: Daizō Shuppan, 1990.

———. *Hongaku shisō hihan* [A Critique of the Doctrine of Original Enlightenment]. Tokyo: Daizō Shuppan, 1989.

Hathaway, Ronald F. *Hierarchy and the Definition of Order in the Letters of Pseudo-Dionysius: A Study in the Form and Meaning of the Pseudo-Dionysian Writings.* The Hague: Nijhoff, 1969.

Heim, S. Mark. *The Depth of the Riches: A Trinitarian Theology of Religious Ends.* Grand Rapids: Eerdmans, 2001.

———. *Faith to Creed: Toward a Common Historical Approach to the Affirmation of the Apostolic Faith in the Fourth Century.* Grand Rapids: Eerdmans, 1991.

———. *Salvations: Truth and Difference in Religion.* Maryknoll: Orbis Books, 1995.

Heisig, James. *Dialogues at One Inch Above the Ground: Reclamations of Belief in an Interreligious Age.* New York: Herder and Herder Crossroad, 2003.

———. *Philosophers of Nothingness: An Essay on the Kyoto School.* Honolulu: University of Hawaii Press, 2001.

Herberg, Will. *Protestant, Catholic, Jew: An Essay in American Religious Sociology.* New York: Doubleday, 1960.

Heschel, Abraham Joshua. *Man is Not Alone.* New York: Farrar, Straus, and Giroux, 1951.

Hick, John. *An Interpretation of Religion: Human Responses to the Transcendent.* New Haven: Yale University Press, 1989.

Hoffner, Eric. *The True Believer: Thoughts on the Nature of Mass Movements.* New York: Harper and Row, 1951.

Hoyland, Robert G. *Seeing Islam as Others Saw It: A Survey and Evaluation of Christian, Jewish and Zoroastrian Writings of Early Islam.* Princeton: Darwin Press, 1997.

Hubbard, Jamie, and Paul L. Swanson, eds. *Pruning the Bodhi Tree: The Storm over Critical Buddhism.* Honolulu: University of Hawaii Press, 1997.

Huntington, C.W. *The Emptiness of Emptiness.* Honolulu: University of Hawaii Press, 1989.

Jackson, Roger R., and John J. Makransky, eds. *Buddhist Theology: Critical Reflections by Contemporary Buddhist Scholars.* Surrey: Curzon, 2000.

John Paul II, Pope. *Crossing the Threshold of Hope.* New York: Knopf, 1994.

Kaplan, Stephen. *Different Paths, Different Summits: A Model for Religious Pluralism.* Lanham: Rowman & Littlefield, 2002.

Karsh, Efraim. *Islamic Imperialism: A History.* New Haven: Yale University Press, 2007.

Kasimow, Harold, John P. Keenan, and Linda Klepinger Keenan, eds. *Beside Still Waters: Jews, Christians, and the Way of the Buddha.* Boston: Wisdom Publications, 2003.

Katz, Steven T. "The 'Conservative' Character of Mystical Experience." In *Mysticism and Religious Traditions,* edited by Steven T. Katz, 3–60. Oxford: Oxford University Press, 1983.

Keenan, John P. "Emptiness as a Paradigm for Understanding World Religions." *Buddhist-Christian Studies* 16 (1996): 57–64.

———. *How Master Mou Removes Our Doubts: A Reader-Response Study and Translation of the Mou-tzu Li-huo lun.* Albany: State University of New York Press, 1994.

———. "The Limits of Thomas Merton's Understanding of Buddhism." In *Merton & Buddhism: Wisdom, Emptiness, & Everyday Mind,* edited by Bonnie Bowman Thurston, 118–33. Louisville: Fons Vitae, 2007.

———. *The Meaning of Christ: A Mahāyāna Theology.* Maryknoll: Orbis Books, 1989.

Bibliography

———. "The New Interfaith Context and Shifting Agenda for Religious Thinking." *Interreligious Insight* 1:2 (2003): 27–36.

———, trans. *The Scripture on the Explication of Underlying Meaning (Samdhinirmocana-sūtra)*. Berkeley: Numata Center of Buddhist Translation and Research, 2000.

———. *The Wisdom of James: Parallels with Mahāyāna Buddhism*. New York/Mahwah: The Newman Press, 2005.

Kiyota, Minoru, ed. *Mahāyāna Buddhist Meditation: Theory and Practice*. Honolulu: University of Hawaii Press, 1978.

Knitter, Paul F. *Introducing Theologies of Religions*. Maryknoll: Orbis Books, 2002.

———. *Jesus and the Other Names: Christian Mission and Global Responsibility*. Maryknoll: Orbis Books, 1996.

———. *No Other Name?: A Critical Survey of Christian Attitudes Toward the World Religions*. Maryknoll: Orbis Books, 1985.

———. *One Earth, Many Religions: Multifaith Dialogue and Global Responsibility*. Maryknoll: Orbis Books, 1995.

Lai, Pan-Chiu. "A Mahāyāna Reading of Chalcedon Christology: A Chinese Response to John Keenan." *Buddhist-Christian Studies* 24 (2002): 209–28.

Lindbeck, George A. *The Nature of Doctrine: Religion and Theology in a Postliberal Age*. Philadelphia: Westminster Press, 1984.

Lonergan, Bernard J.F. "Cognitional Structure." *Continuum* 2.3 (1964): 530–42.

———. *Collected Works of Bernard Lonergan*. Vol. 2, *Verbum: Word and Idea in Aquinas*. Toronto: University of Toronto Press, 1997.

———. *Doctrinal Pluralism*. Milwaukee: Marquette University Press, 1971.

———. *Insight: A Study of Human Understanding*. London: Longmans, Green and Co., New York: Philosophical Library, 1957. Reissued in *Collected Works of Bernard Lonergan*, vol 3. Toronto: University of Toronto Press, 1992.

———. *Method in Theology*. New York: Herder and Herder, 1972.

———. *A Second Collection*. Philadelphia: Westminster Press, 1974.

Loy, David R. *Awareness Bound and Unbound: Reflecting and Refracting Buddhism*. Forthcoming from State University of New York Press.

———. *The Great Awakening: A Buddhist Social Theory*. Boston: Wisdom, 2003.

———. *Lack and Transcendence: The Problem of Life and Death in Psychotherapy, Existentialism, and Buddhism*. Amherst: Humanity Books, 1996.

Lusthaus, Dan. *Buddhist Phenomenology: A Philosophical Investigation of Yogācāra Buddhism and the Ch'eng Wei-shih lun*. London: Routledge Curzon, 2002.

Makransky, John J. *Buddhahood Embodied: Sources of Controversy in India and Tibet*. Albany: State University of New York Press, 1997.

Martel, Yann. *The Life of Pi: A Novel*. Toronto: Vintage Canada, 2001.

May, Jacques. *Candrakīrti: Prasannapadā Madhyamikavṛtti. Douze chapitres traduits du Sanskrit et du Tibétain, accompagnés d'une introduction, de notes, et d'une edition critique de la version Tibétaine*. Paris: Adrien-Maisonneuve, 1959.

Meyendorff, John. *Christ in Eastern Christian Thought*. New York: St. Vladimir's Press, 1975.

———. "The Nicene Creed: Uniting or Dividing Confession?" In *Faith to Creed: Towards a Common Historical Approach to the Affirmation of the Apostolic Faith in the Fourth Century*, edited by S. Mark Heim, 1–19. Grand Rapids: Eerdmans, 1991.

Muck, Terry. *The Mysterious Beyond*. Grand Rapids: Baker Books, 1993.

Bibliography

Nagao, Gadjin. *The Foundational Standpoint of Mādhyamika Philosophy*. Translated by John P. Keenan. Albany: State University of New York Press, 1989.

———. *Shōdaijōron: wayaku to chūkai* [Mahāyānasaṃgraha: Japanese Translation and Notes]. 2 vols. Tokyo: Kodansha, 1982, 1987.

———. "The Silence of the Buddha and its Madhyamic Interpretation." In *Mādhyamika and Yogācāra: A Study of Mahāyāna Philosophies*, edited by Leslie Kawamura, 35–50. Albany: State University of New York Press, 1991.

Nāgārjuna. *Mūlamadhyamakakārikah* [Stanzas on the Middle]. Sanskrit text edited by J. W. de Jong. Madras: Adyar Library and Research Center, 1977. [For an English translation, see Kenneth Inada, *Nāgārjuna: A Translation of his Mūlamadhyamakakārikah*. Tokyo: Hokuseido, 1970].

Newland, Guy. *The Two Truths*. Ithaca, NY: Snow Lion Publications, 1992.

Nhat Hanh, Thich. *The Diamond That Cuts Through Illusion: Commentaries on the Prajnaparmita Diamond Sūtra*. Berkeley: Parallax Press, 1992.

———. *Going Home: Jesus and Buddha as Brothers*. New York: Riverhead Books, 1999.

Nietzsche, Friedrich. *Thus Spoke Zarathustra*. Translated by Walter Kaufmann. New York: Penguin Books, 1954.

———. *The Will to Power*. Translated by Walter Kaufmann. New York: Vintage Books, 1967.

Nishitani, Keiji. *Religion and Nothingness*. Translated by Jan van Bragt. Berkeley: University of California Press, 1982.

Niwano, Nikkyō. *Buddhism for Today: A Modern Interpretation of the Threefold Lotus Sutra*. New York: Weatherhill, Tokyo: Kosei, 1961.

———. *A Guide to the Threefold Lotus Sutra*. Tokyo: Kosei, 1981.

———. "The Realm of the One Vehicle." *Dharma World* (January–March 2007): 43.

O'Leary, Joseph S. "Emptiness and Dogma." *Japan Mission Journal* (Winter 2001): 227–45.

———. *Questioning Back: Overcoming Metaphysics in Christian Tradition*. Minneapolis: Winston Press, 1986.

———. "Religions as Conventions." In *The Blackwell Companion of Postmodern Theology*, edited by Graham Ward, 413–24. Oxford: Oxford University Press, 2001.

———. *Religious Pluralism and Christian Truth*. Edinburgh: Edinburgh University Press, 1996.

Pelikan, Jaroslav. *The Christian Tradition: A History of the Development of Doctrine*. 5 vols. Chicago: University of Chicago Press, 1983.

———. *Credo: Historical and Theological Guide to Creeds and Confessions of Faith in the Christian Tradition*. New Haven: Yale University Press, 2003.

———. *Jesus Through the Centuries: His Place in the History of Culture*. New Haven: Yale University Press, 1985.

Pickering, W.S.F. *Durkheim's Sociology of Religion*. London: Routledge and Kegan Paul, 1999.

Queen, Christopher S. and Sallie B. King, eds. *Engaged Buddhism: Buddhist Liberation Movements in Asia*. Albany: State University of New York Press, 1996.

Race, Alan. *Christians and Religious Pluralism: Patterns in the Christian Theology of Religions*. Maryknoll: Orbis Books, 1983.

Radhakrishnan, Sarvepalli. *Eastern Religions and Western Thought*. Oxford: Oxford University, 1939.

Bibliography

———. "The Indian Approach to the Religious Problem." In *The Indian Mind: Essentials of Indian Philosophy and Culture*, edited by Charles A. Moore, 173–82. Honolulu: University of Hawaii Press, 1967.

Rahner, Karl. *Nature and Grace and Other Essays.* London: Sheed and Ward, 1963.

———. *Sacramentum Mundi: An Encyclopedia of Theology.* 6 vols. New York: Herder and Herder, 1968.

———. *Theological Investigations.* 22 vols. London: Longman & Todd & Baltimore: Helicon Press, 1961.

Ratzinger, Joseph. *Truth and Tolerance: Christian Belief and World Religions.* San Francisco: Ignatius, 2003.

Roberts, Alexander, and James Donaldson, eds. *Ante-Nicene Fathers.* Revised by A. Cleveland Coxe. 10 vols. Peabody: Hendrickson, 1885, 1995.

Robinson, Richard H. *Early Mādhyamika in India and China.* Madison: University of Wisconsin Press, 1967.

Roy, Louis. *Mystical Consciousness: Western Perspectives and Dialogue with Japanese Thinkers.* Albany: State University of New York Press, 2003.

———. *Transcendent Experiences: Phenomenology and Critique.* Toronto: University of Toronto Press, 2001.

Russell, Mary Doria. *The Children of God.* New York: Fawcett Books, Random House, 1999.

———. *The Sparrow.* New York: Ballantine Books, Random House, 1997.

Said, Edward W. *Orientalism.* New York: Vintage Books, 1997.

Schachter-Shalomi, Rabbi Zalman. "Interview, April 25, 2001." In *Beside Still Waters: Jews, Christians, and the Way of the Buddha*, edited by Harold Kasimow, John P. Keenan, and Linda Klepinger Keenan, 85–98. Boston: Wisdom, 2003.

Schillebeeckx, Edward. *Christ: The Experience of Jesus as Lord.* New York: Seabury Press, 1977.

Schmidt-Leukel, Perry, ed. *Christianity, Buddhism, and the Question of Creation: Karmic or Divine?* Hants, England and Burlington, Vermont: Ashgate Publishing, 2006.

Smith, Jonathan. *Map is Not Territory: Studies in the History of Religions.* Chicago: University of Chicago Press, 1993.

Stace, W.T. *Mysticism and Philosophy.* London: Macmillan, 1960.

Streng, Fredrick J. *Emptiness: A Study in Religious Meaning.* New York: Abingdon Press, 1967.

Suzuki, Daisetsu Teitarō. *Essays In Zen Buddhism.* 3 vols. 1949. Reprint, New York: Grove Press, 1961.

Takasaki, Jikidō. *A Study of the Ratnagotravibhāga (Uttaratantra), Being a Treatise of the Tathāgatagarbha of Mahāyāna Buddhism.* Rome: Istituto italiano per il Medio ed Estremo Oriente,1966.

Takizawa, Katsumi. *Tannishō to Gendai* [The Tannishō and the Modern Age]. Tokyo: San'ichi Shōbō, 1974.

Thomas, Edward J. *The Life of Buddha as Legend and History.* London, Routledge and Kegan Paul, 1975 (first printing 1927).

Tillemans, Tom J.F. *Materials for the Study of Āryadeva, Dharmapāla, and Candrakīrti: The Catuḥśataka of Āryadeva, Chapters XII and XIII With the Commentaries of Dharmapāla and Candrakīrti—Introduction, Translation, Sanskrit, Tibetan and Chinese Texts, Notes.* 2 vols. Wien: Arbeitskreis für Tibetische und Buddhistische Studien Universität Wien, 1990.

Bibliography

Unno, Taitetsu, trans. *Tannishō: A Shin Buddhist Classic*. Honolulu: Buddhist Studies Center Press, 1984 and frequently thereafter.

van Bragt, Jan. "Shoshūkyō taiwa no shomondai" [Problems in Interreligious Dialogue]. In *Shūkyō to bunka* [Religon and Culture], edited by the Nanzan Institute for Religion and Culture. Kyoto: Jimbun Shoin, 1994.

Waldron, William S. *The Buddhist Unconscious: The Ālaya-vijñāna in the Context of Indian Buddhist Thought*. London: Routledge Curzon, 2003.

Watson, Burton, trans. *The Lotus Sūtra*. New York: Columbia University Press, 1993.

Wayman, Alex and Hideko. *The Lion's Roar of Queen Śrīmālā: A Buddhist Scripture of the Tathāgatagarbha Tradition*. New York: Columbia, 1974.

Williams, Rowan. "The Finality of Jesus Christ." In *On Christian Theology*. London: Blackwell, 2000.

Made in the USA
Monee, IL
14 March 2024

55041568R00075